We hope you enjoy coloring this book.

Download some extra

free coloring patterns

and get news of upcoming books at

www.scribblepresscoloring.com/free-download

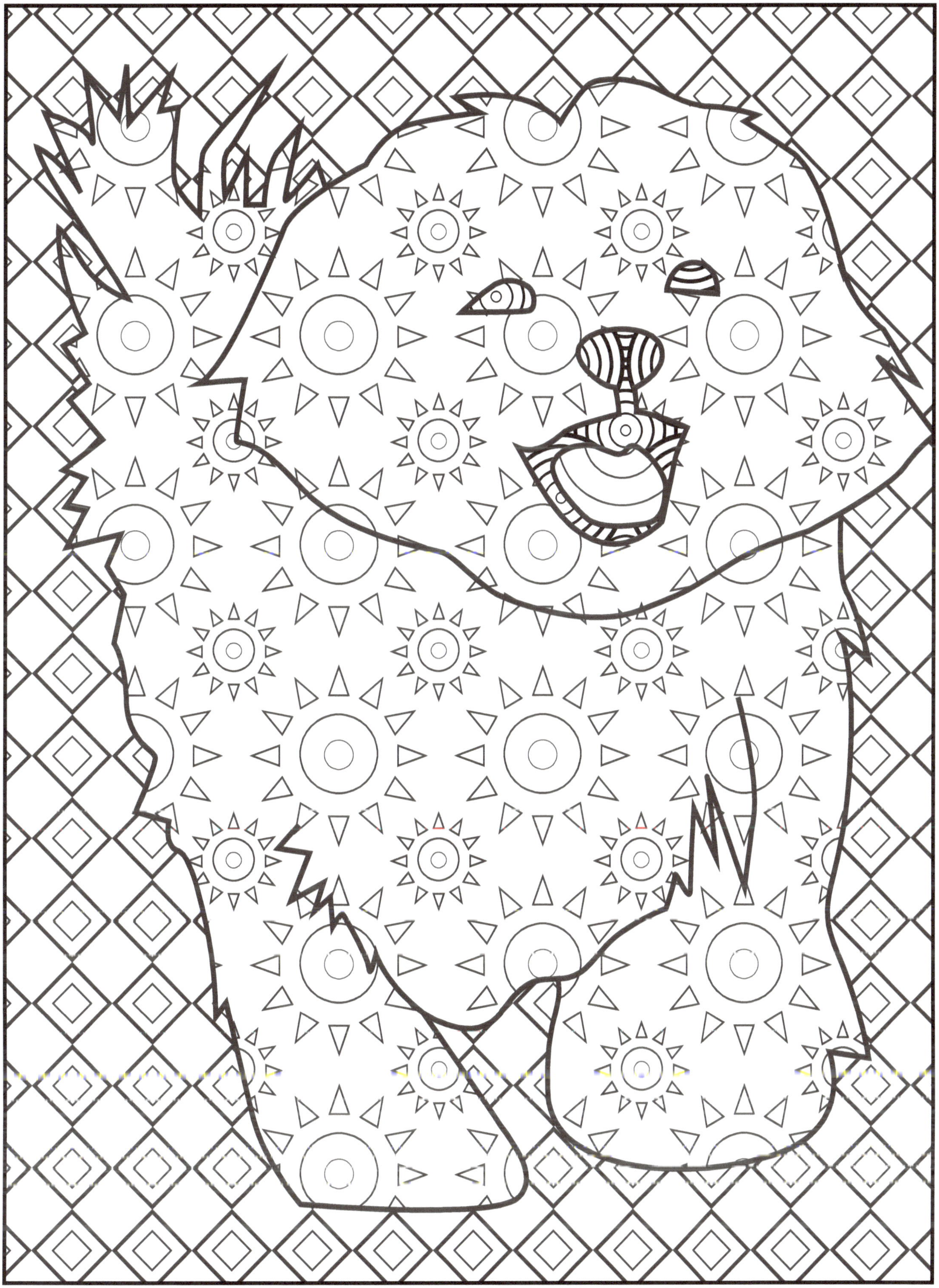

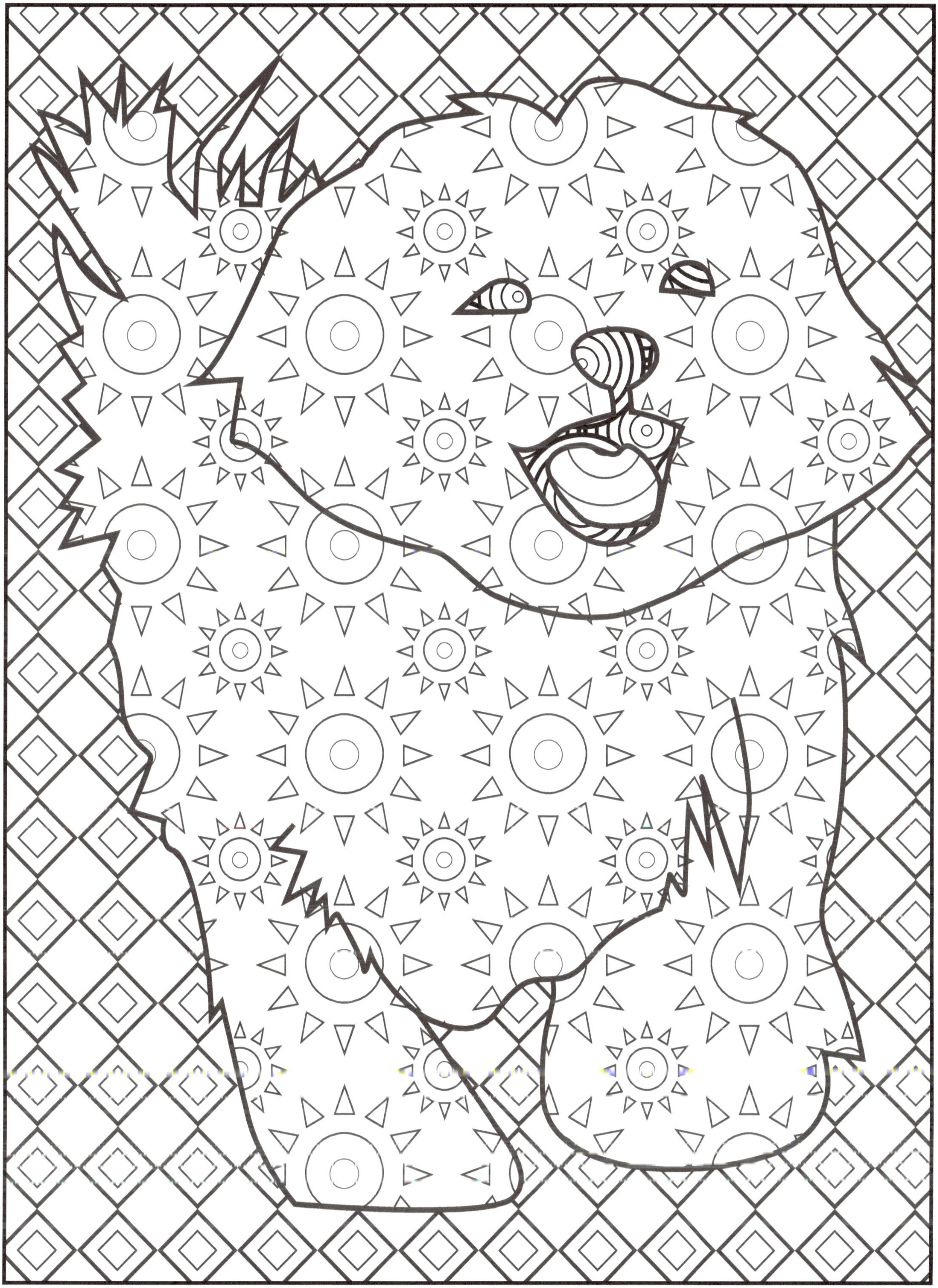

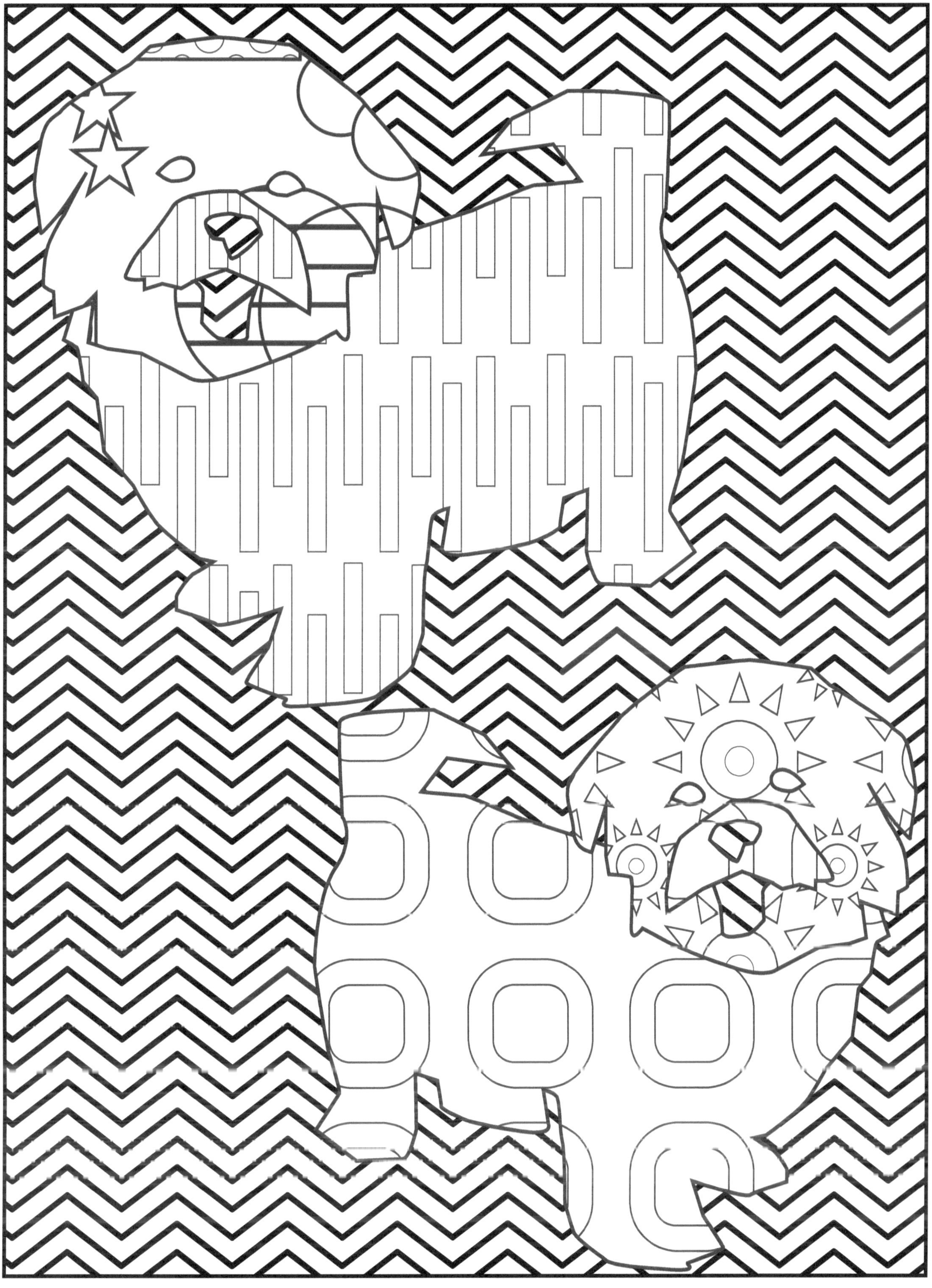

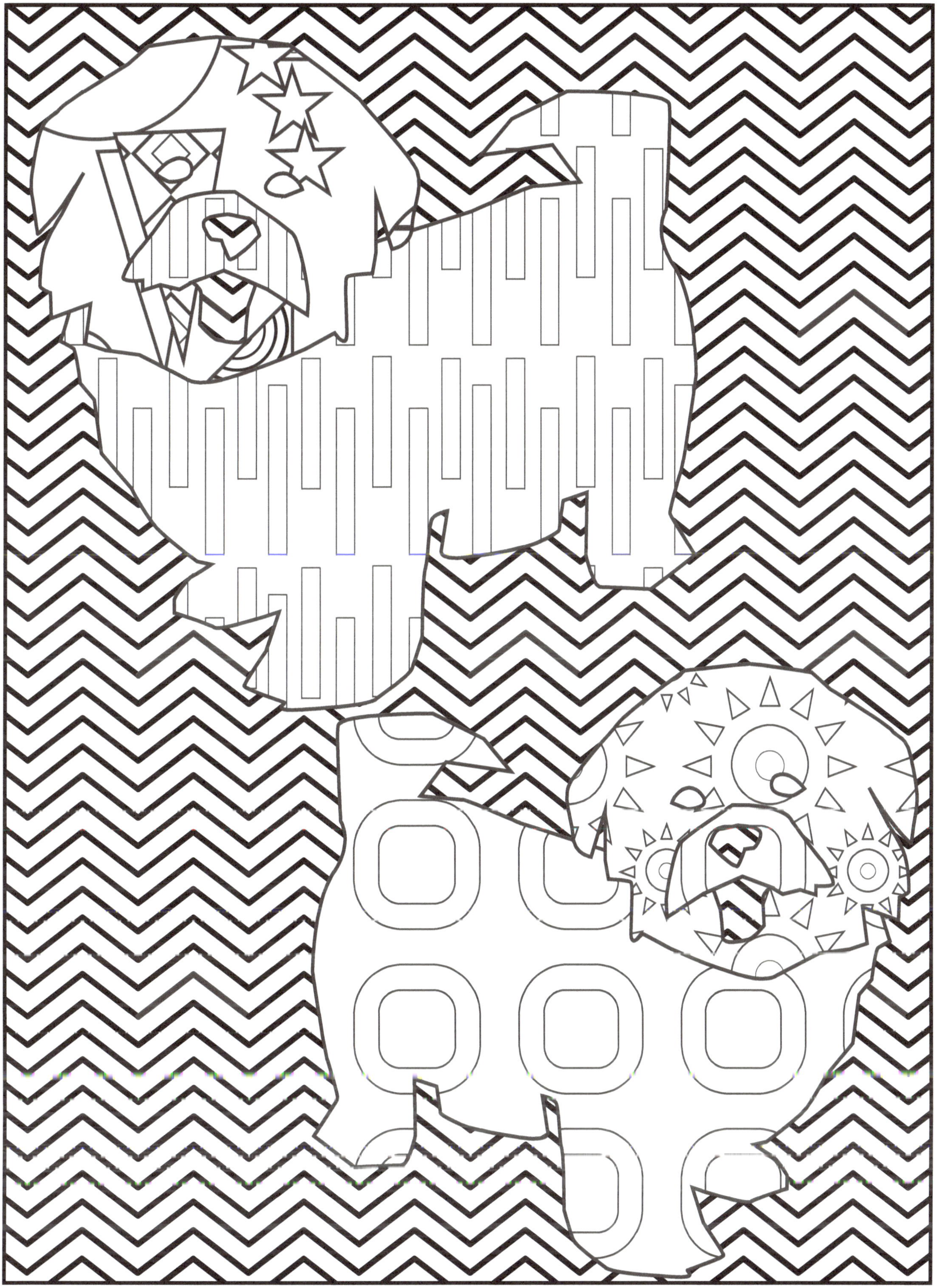

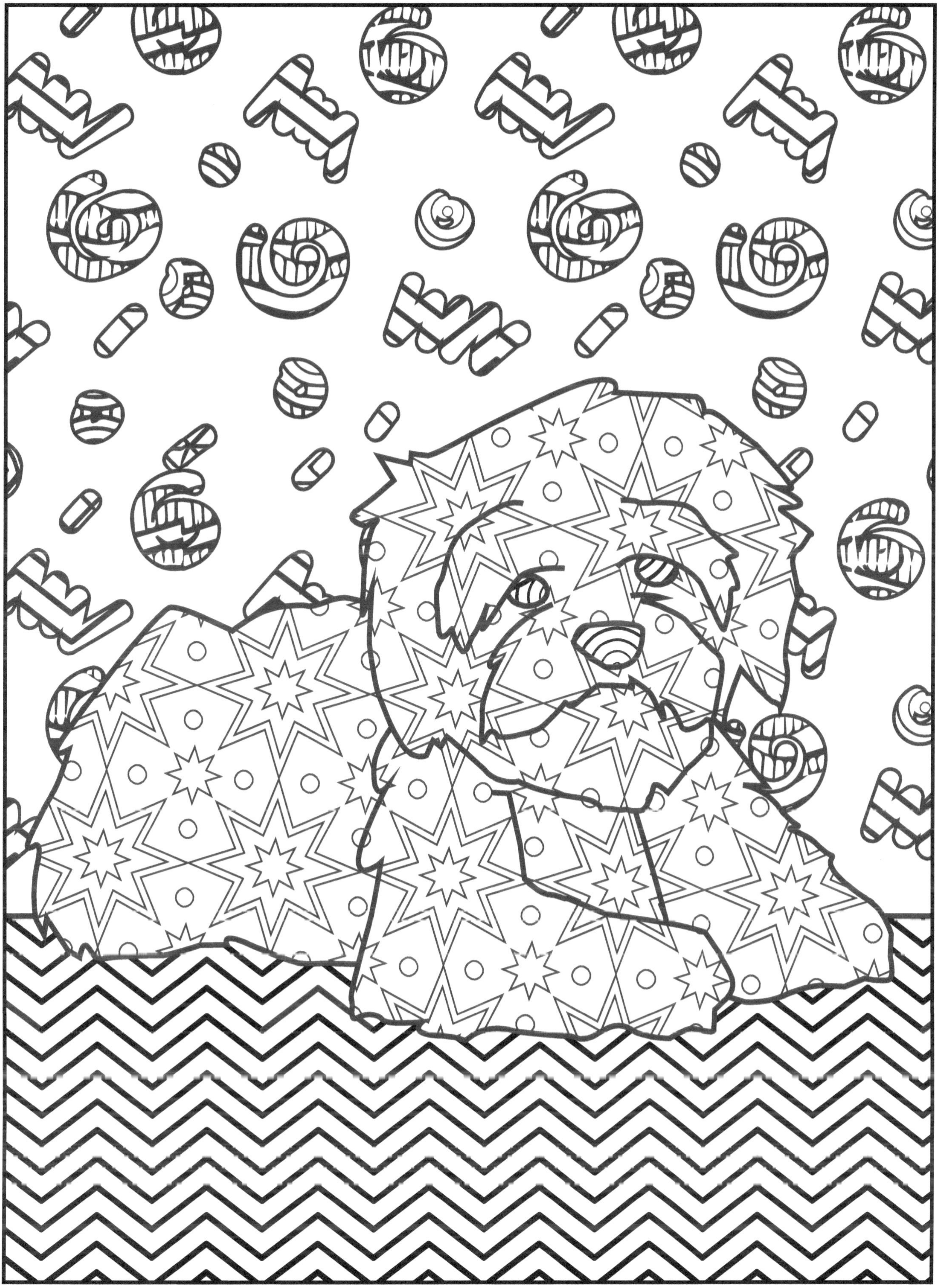

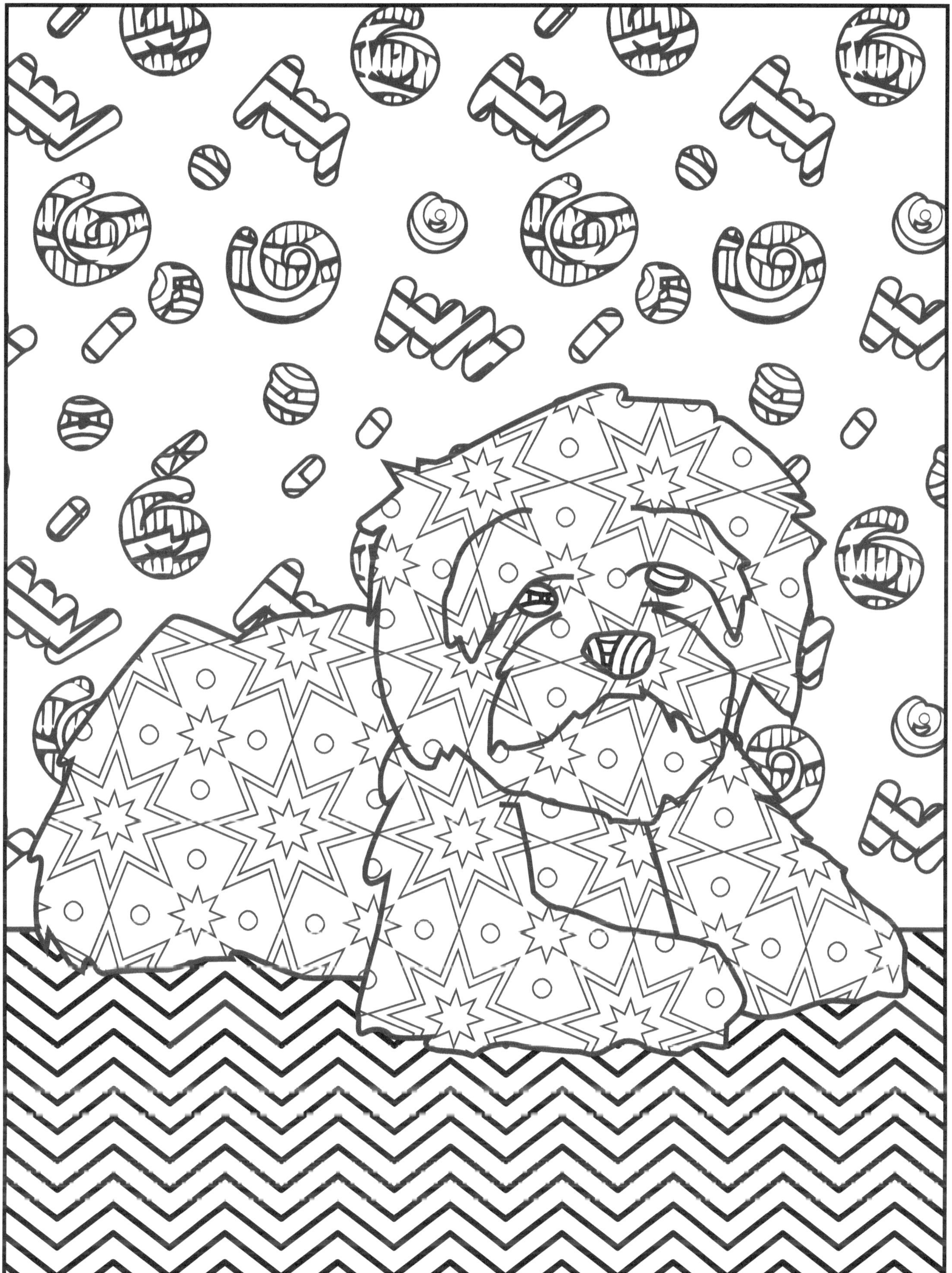

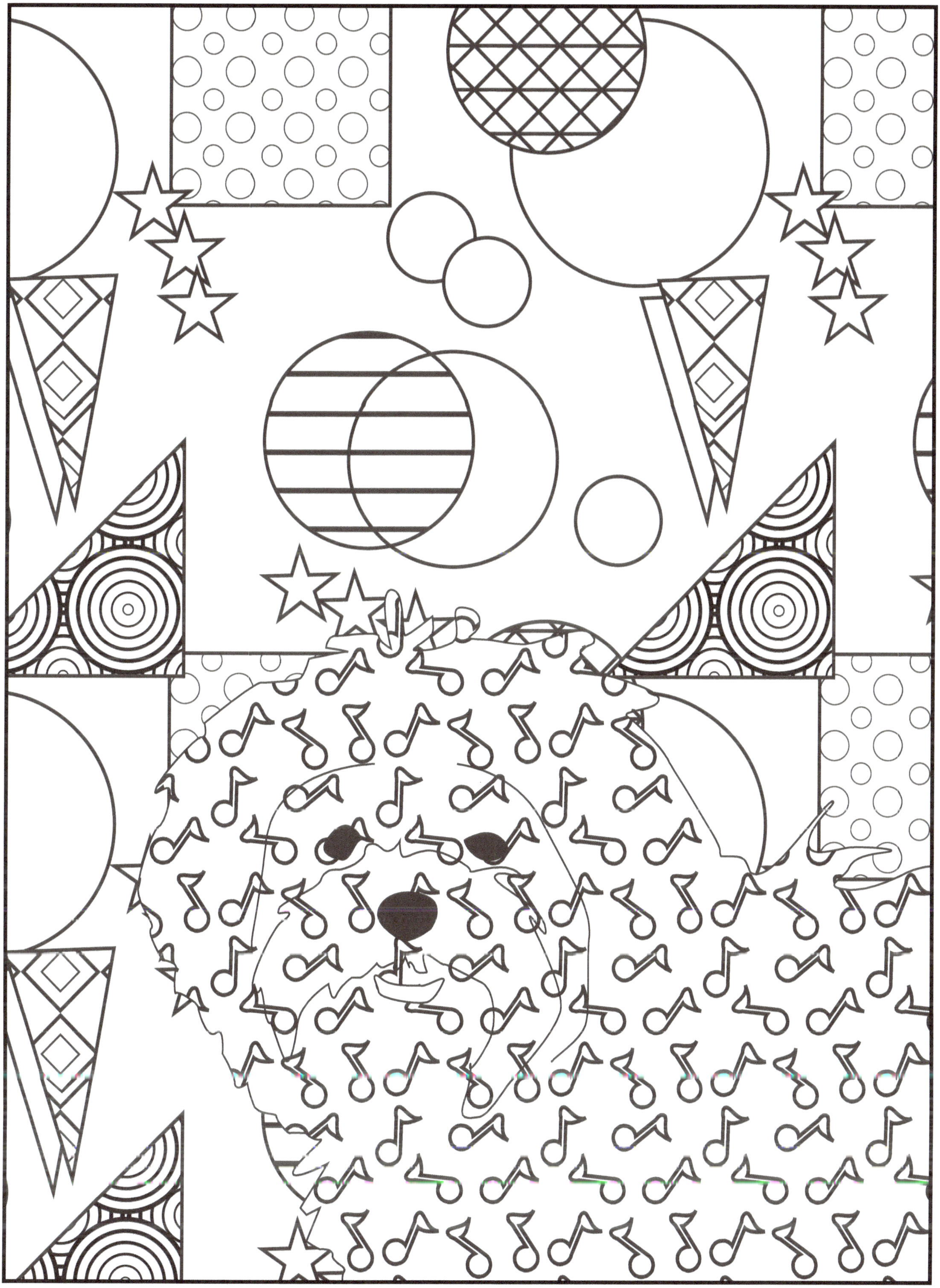

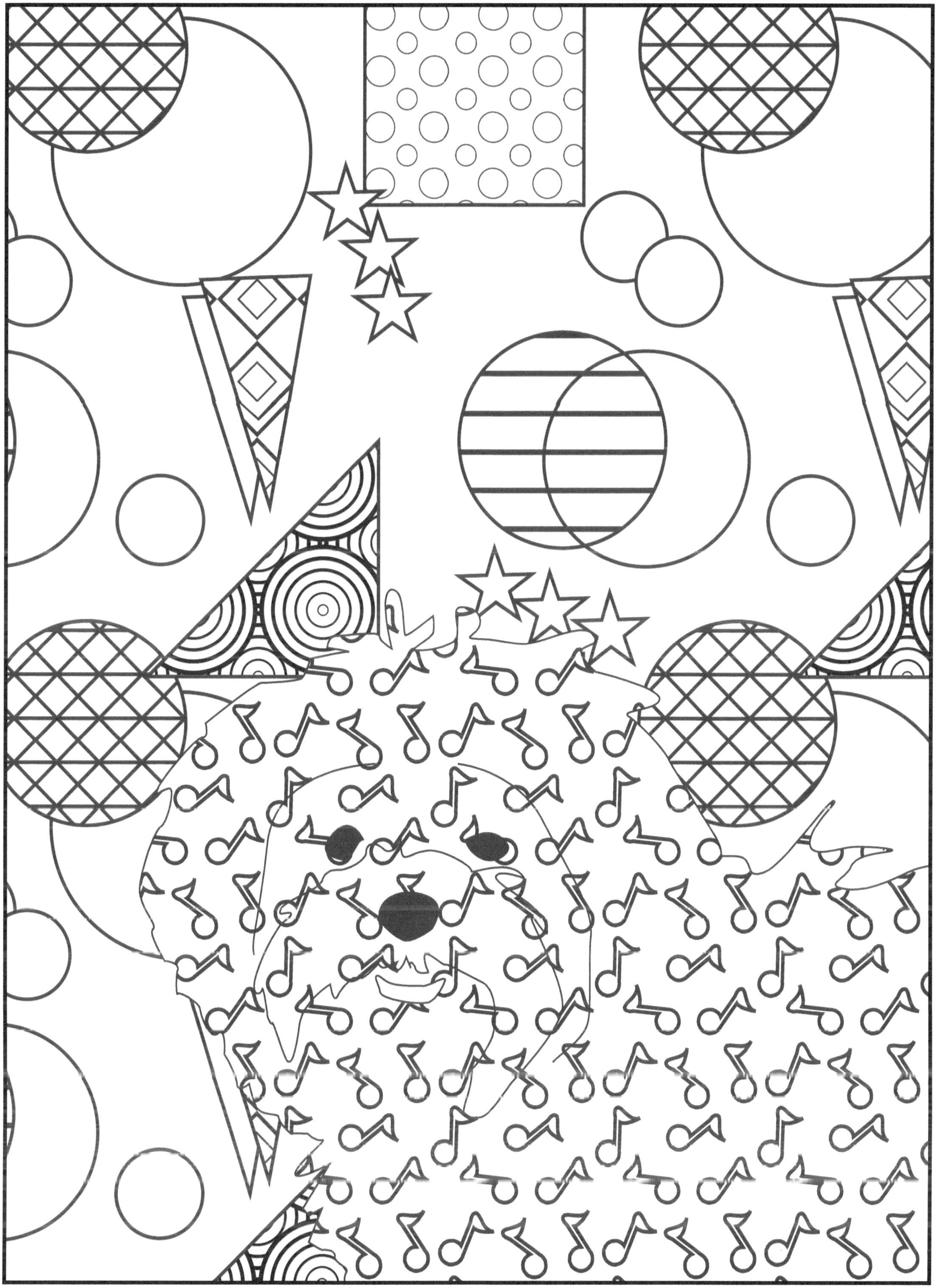

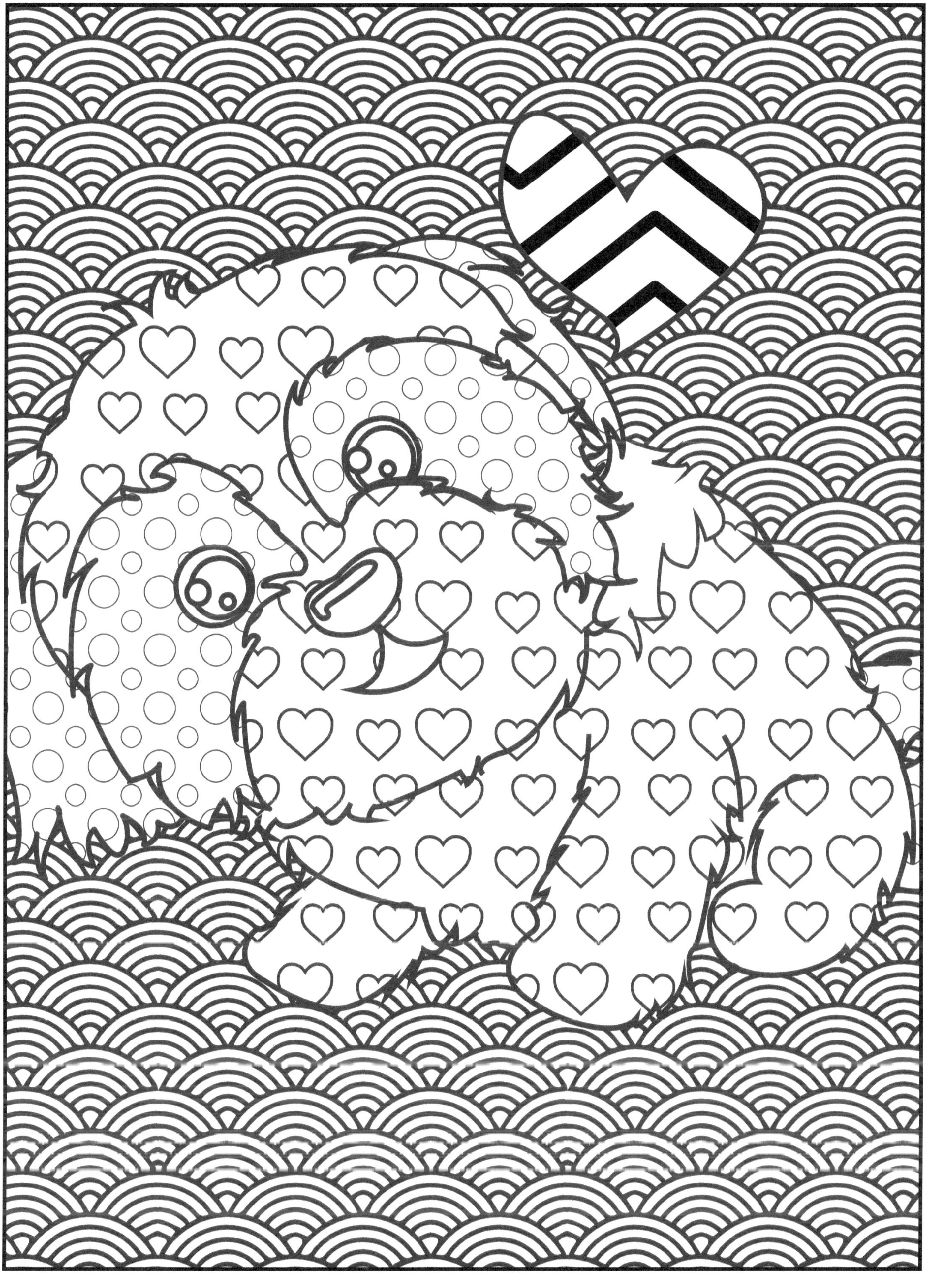

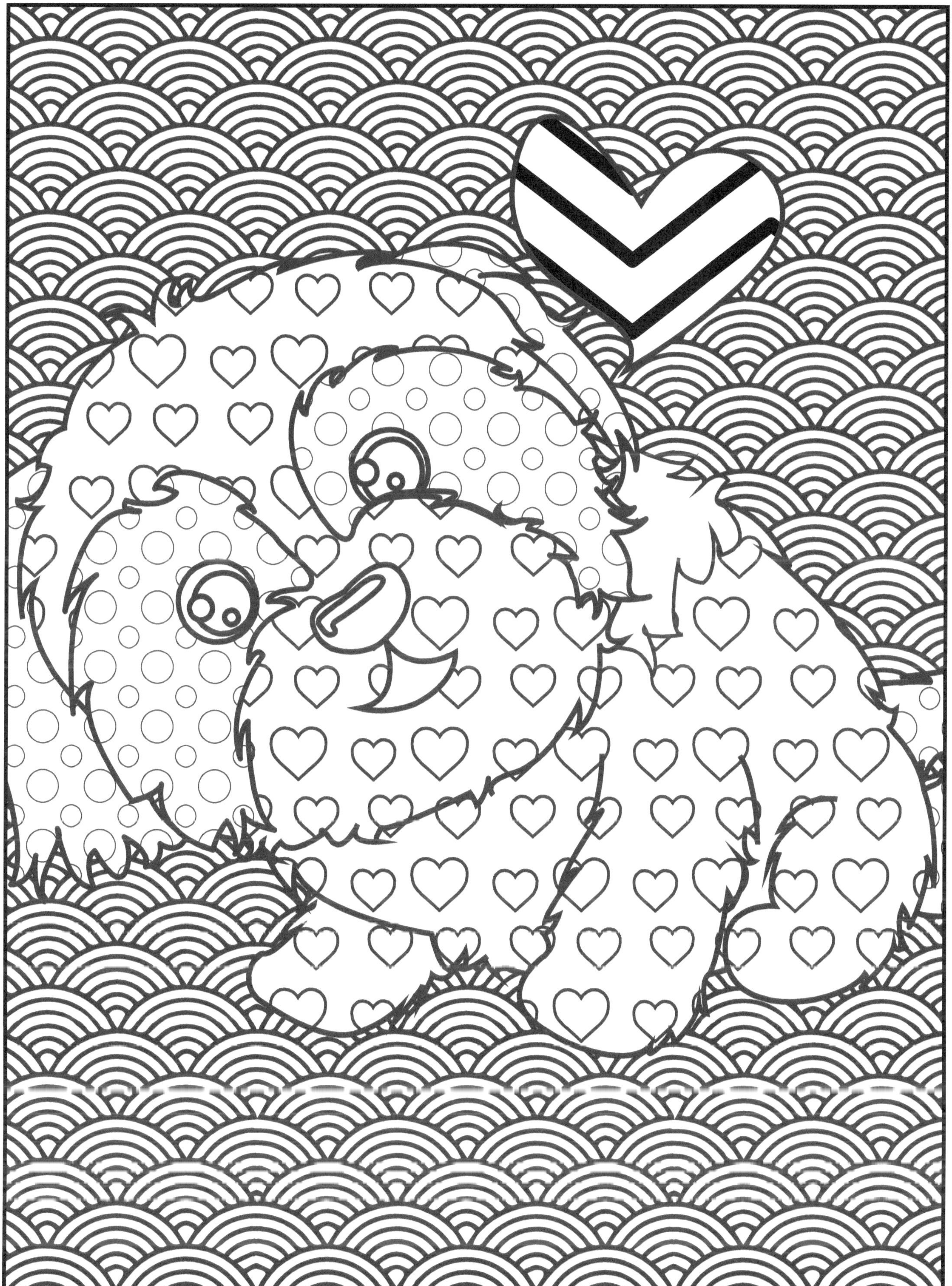

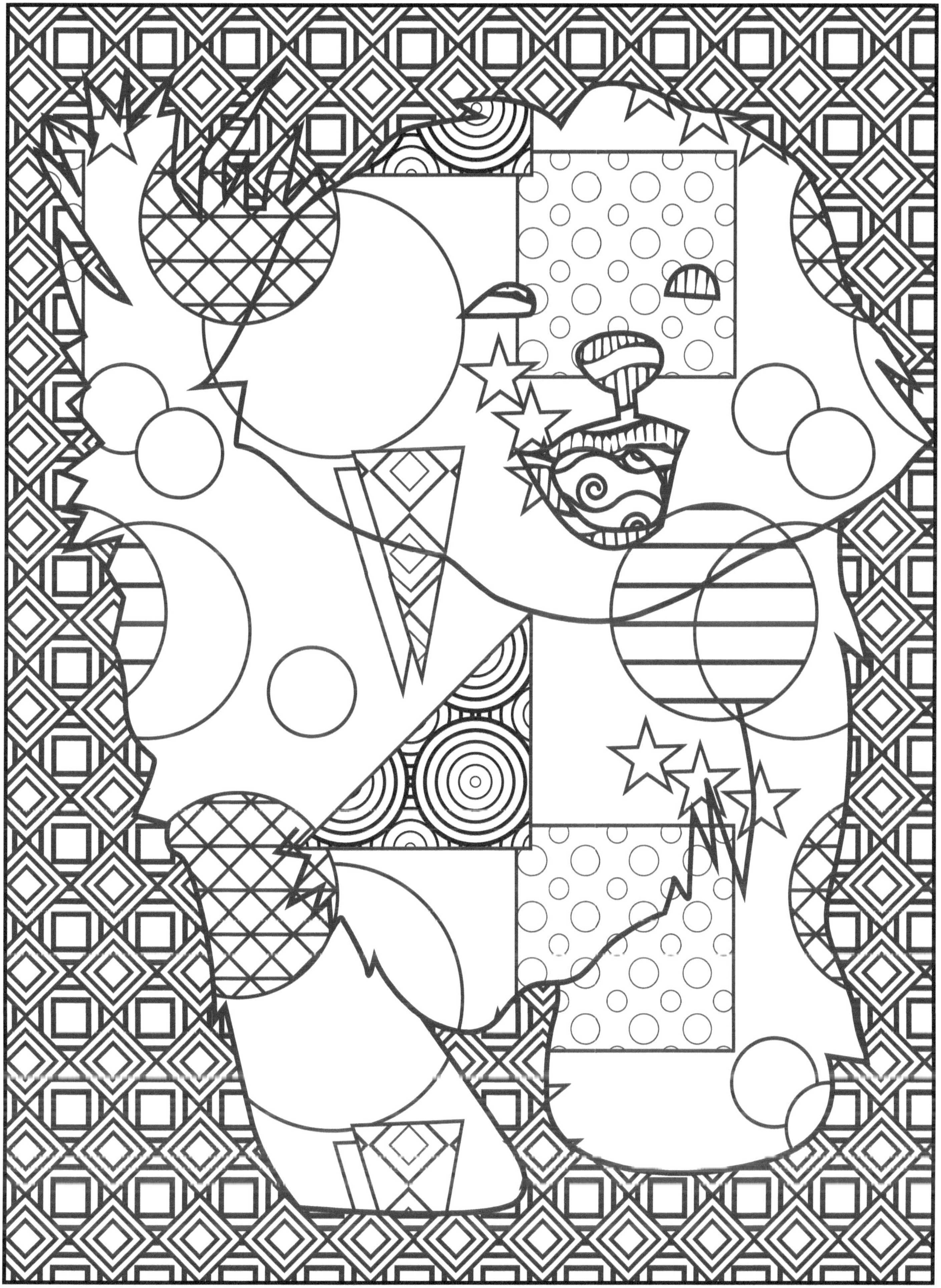

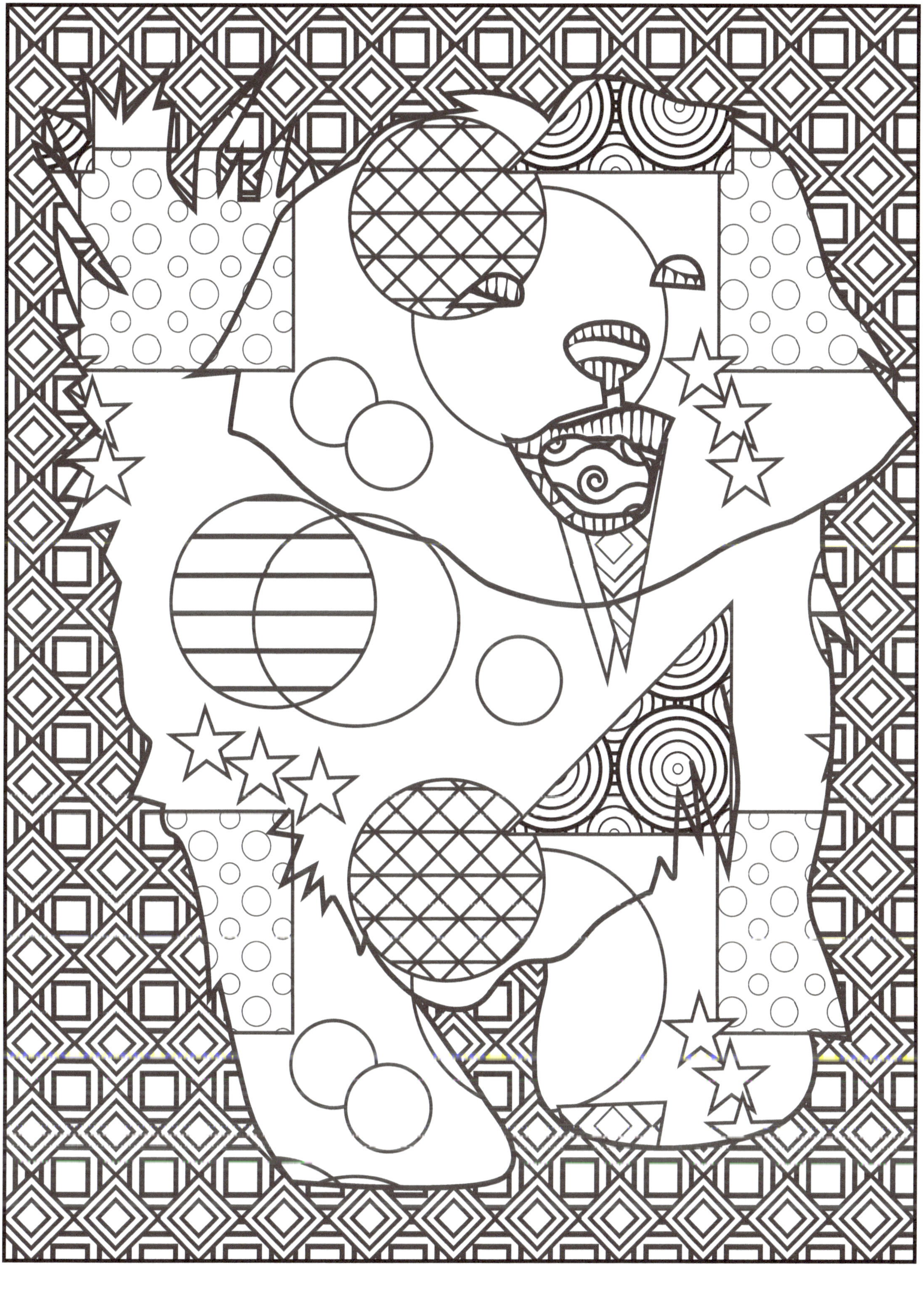

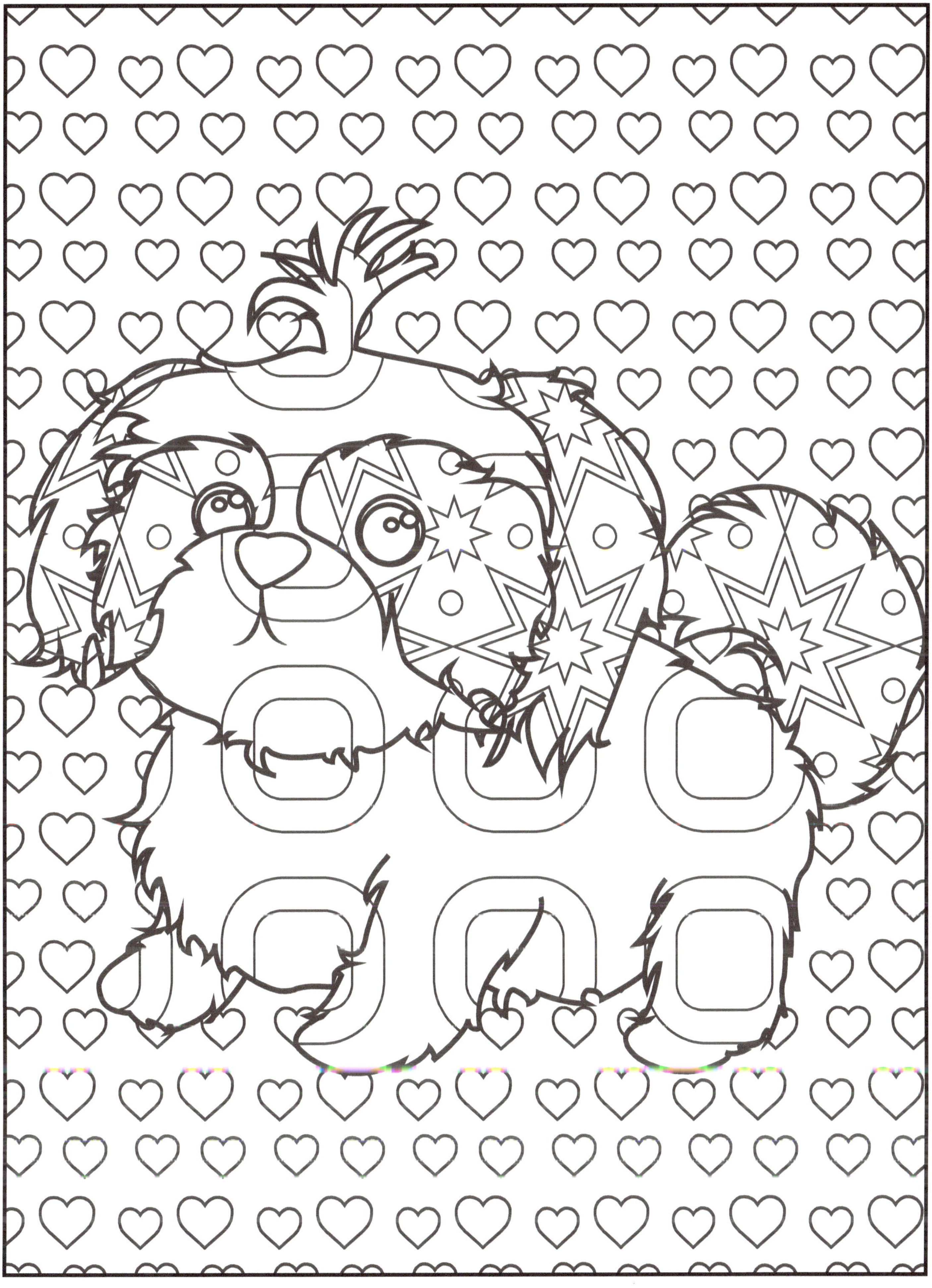

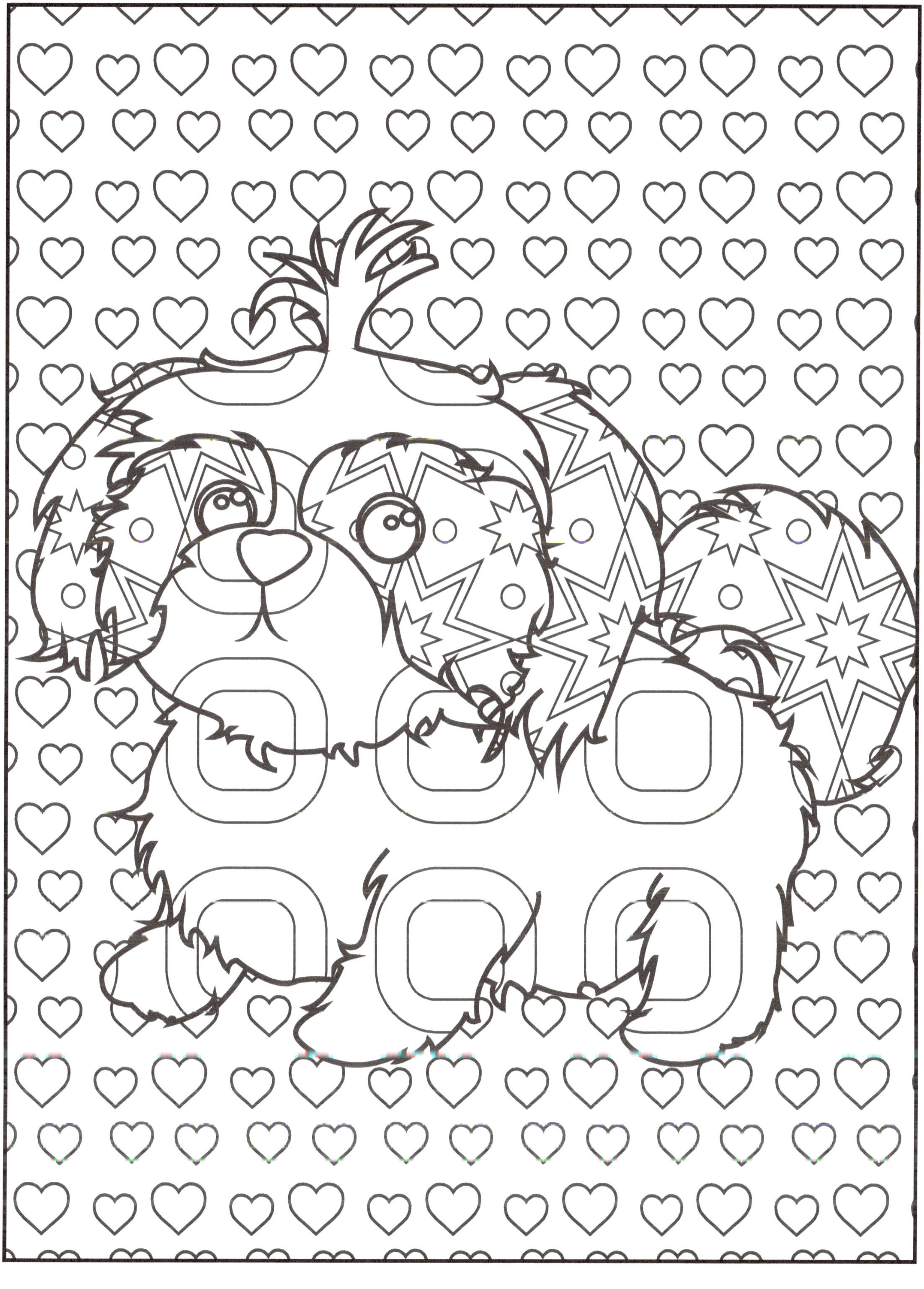

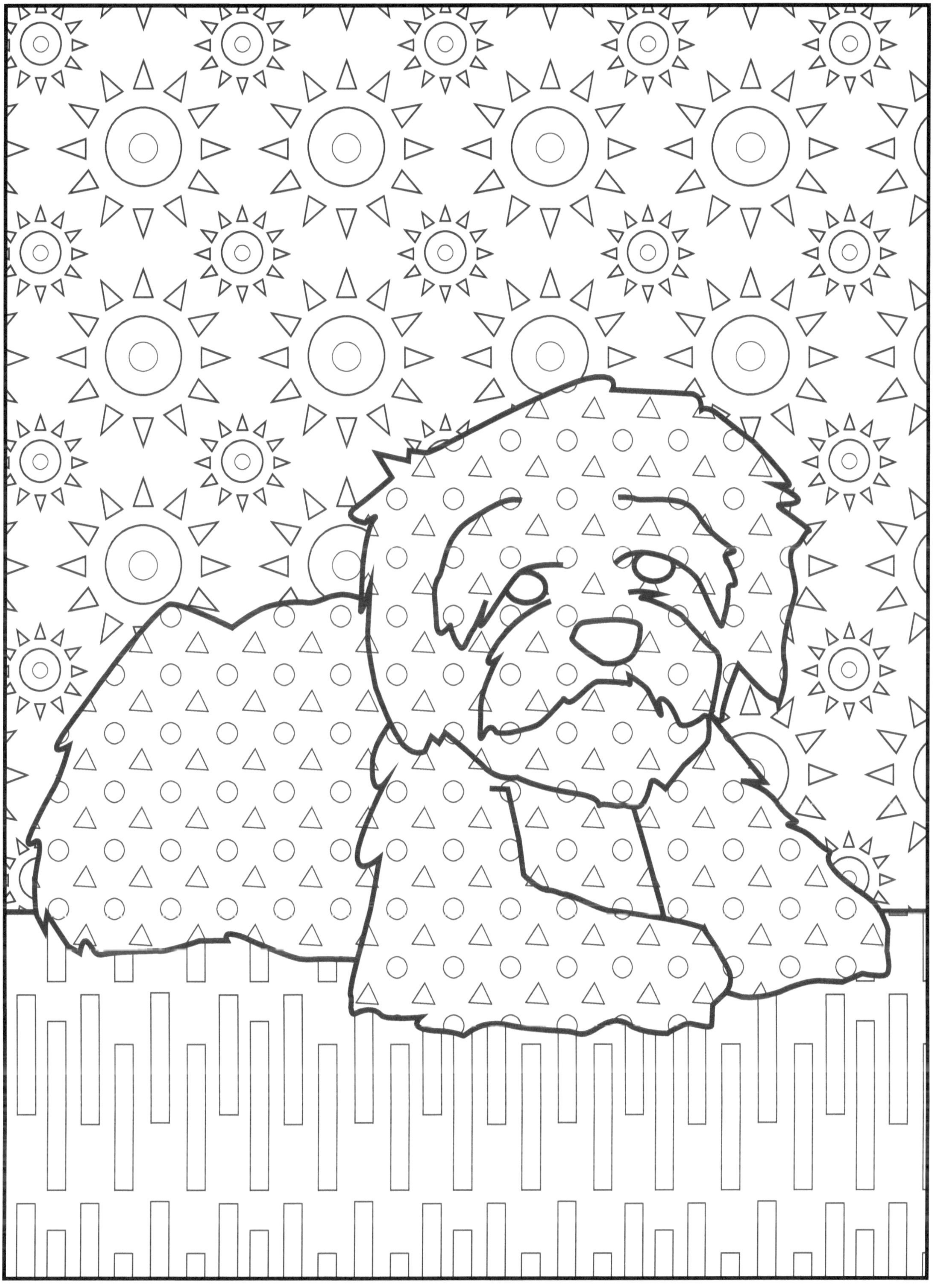

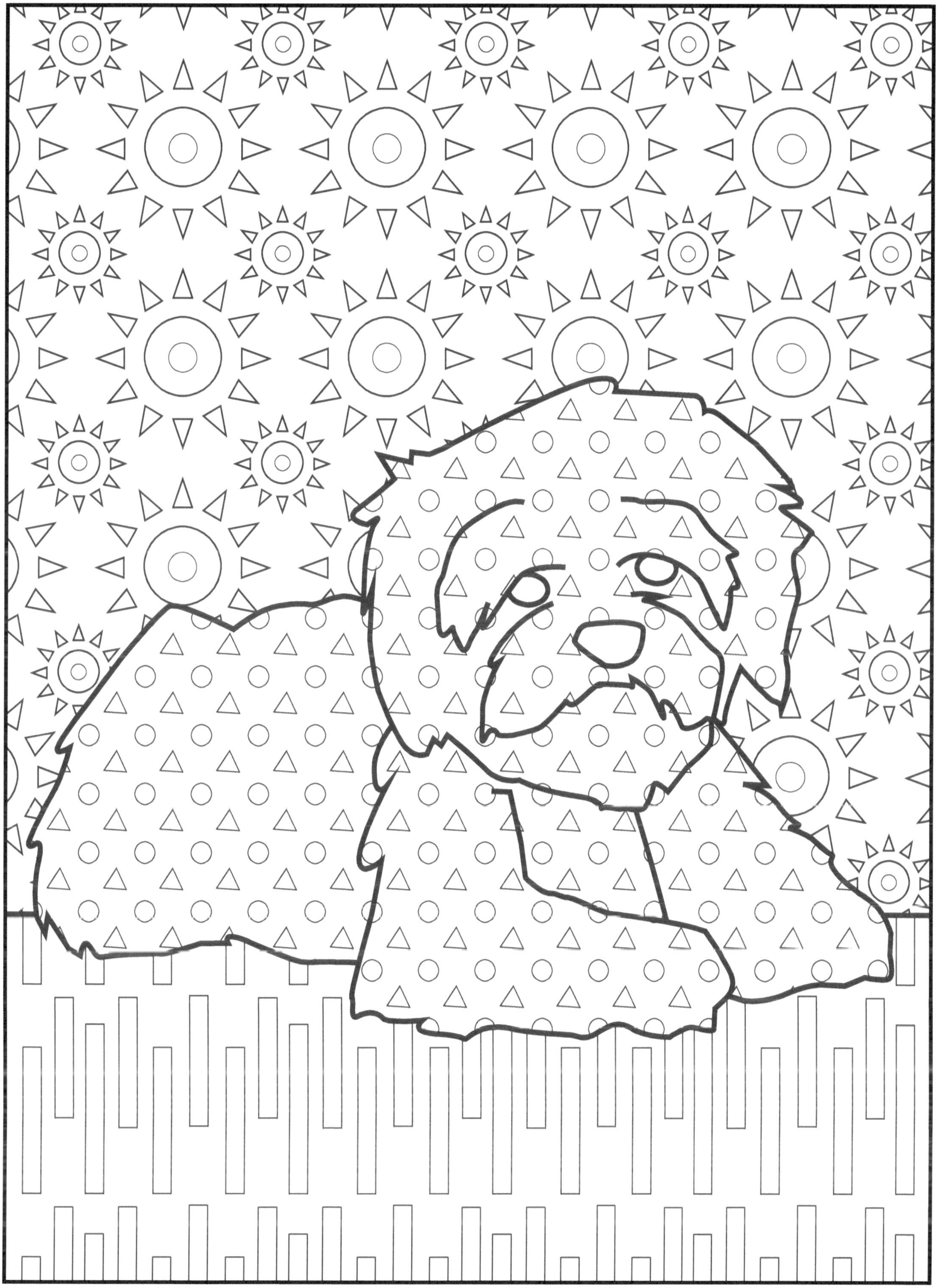

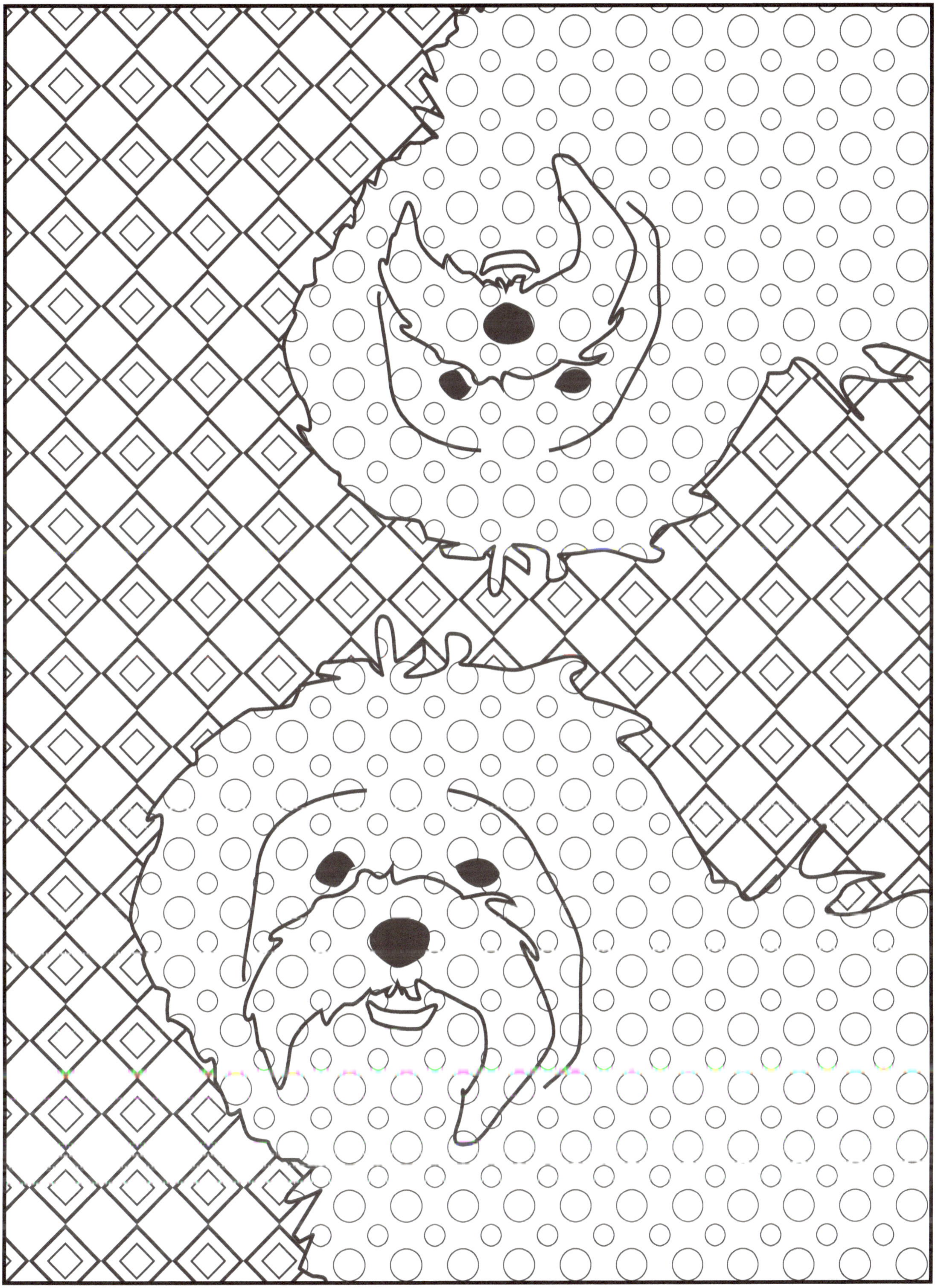

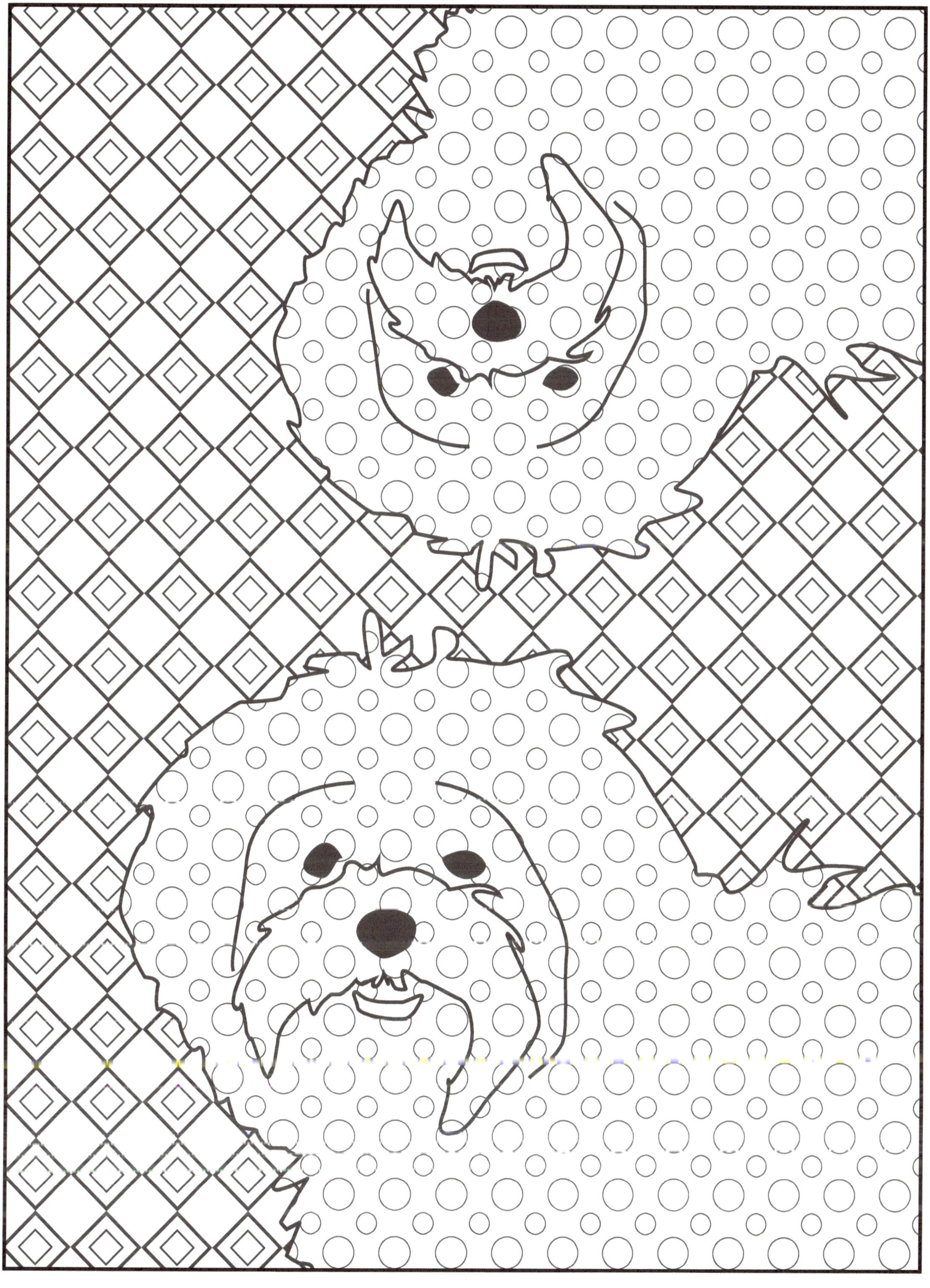

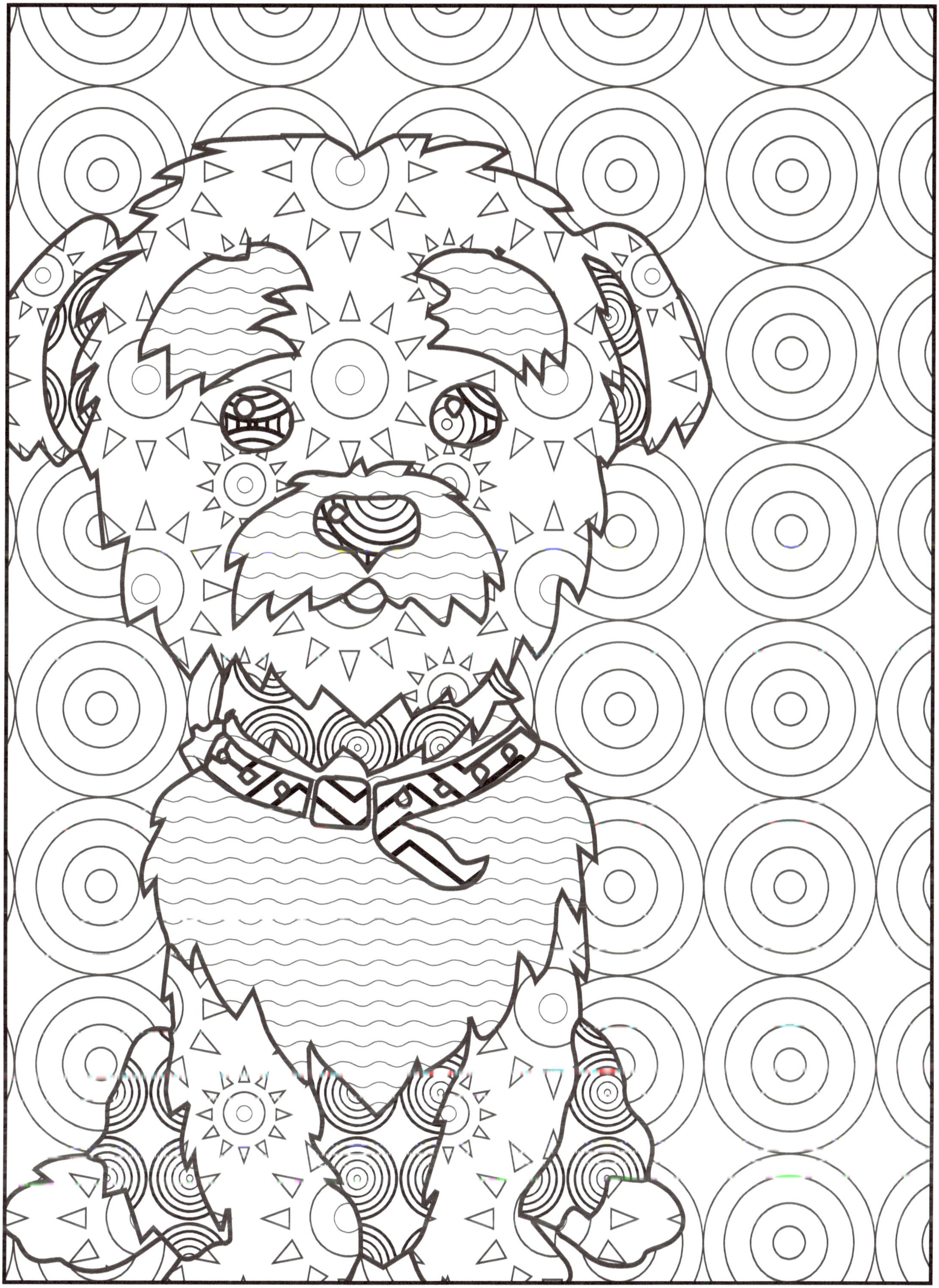

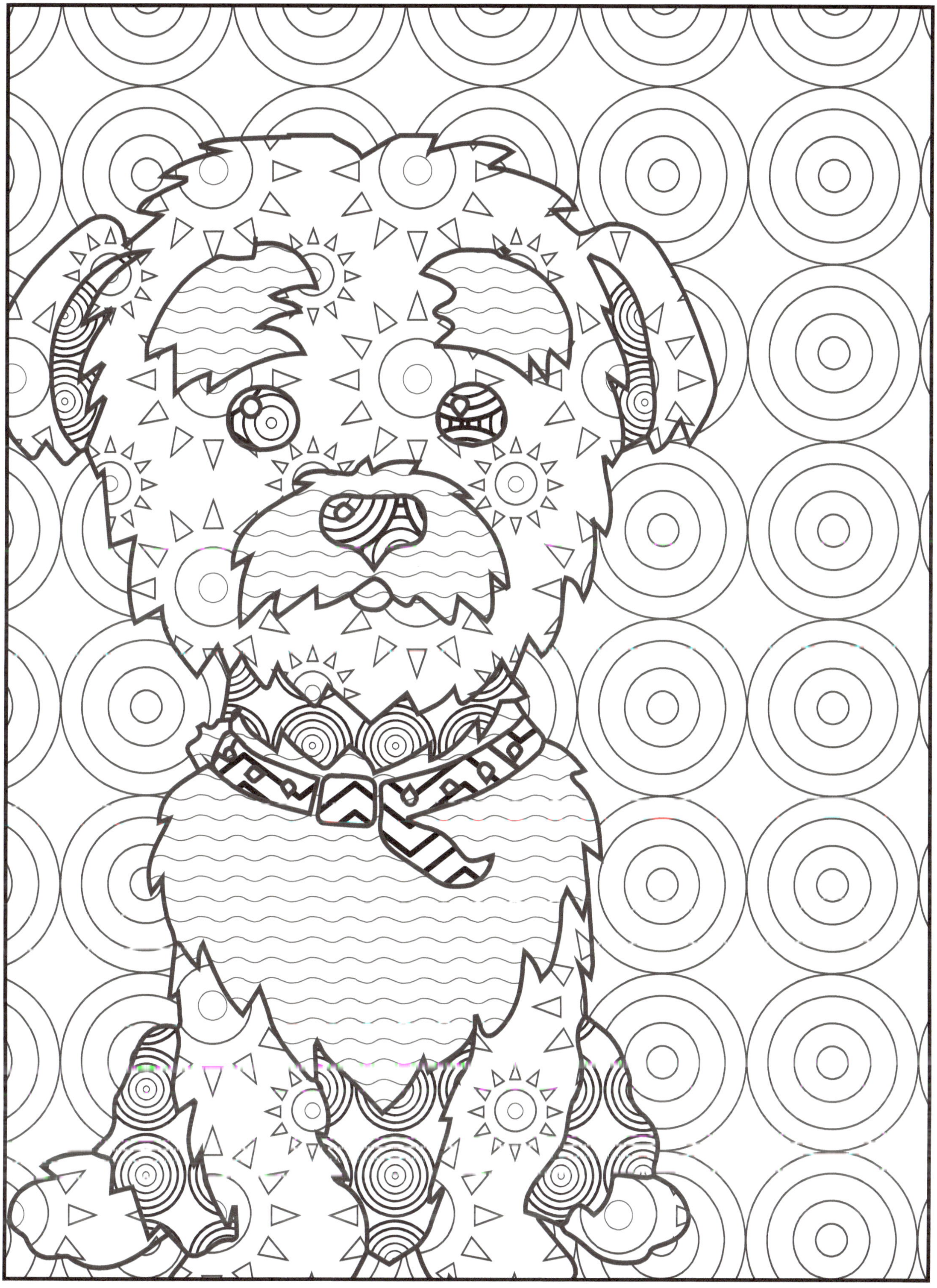

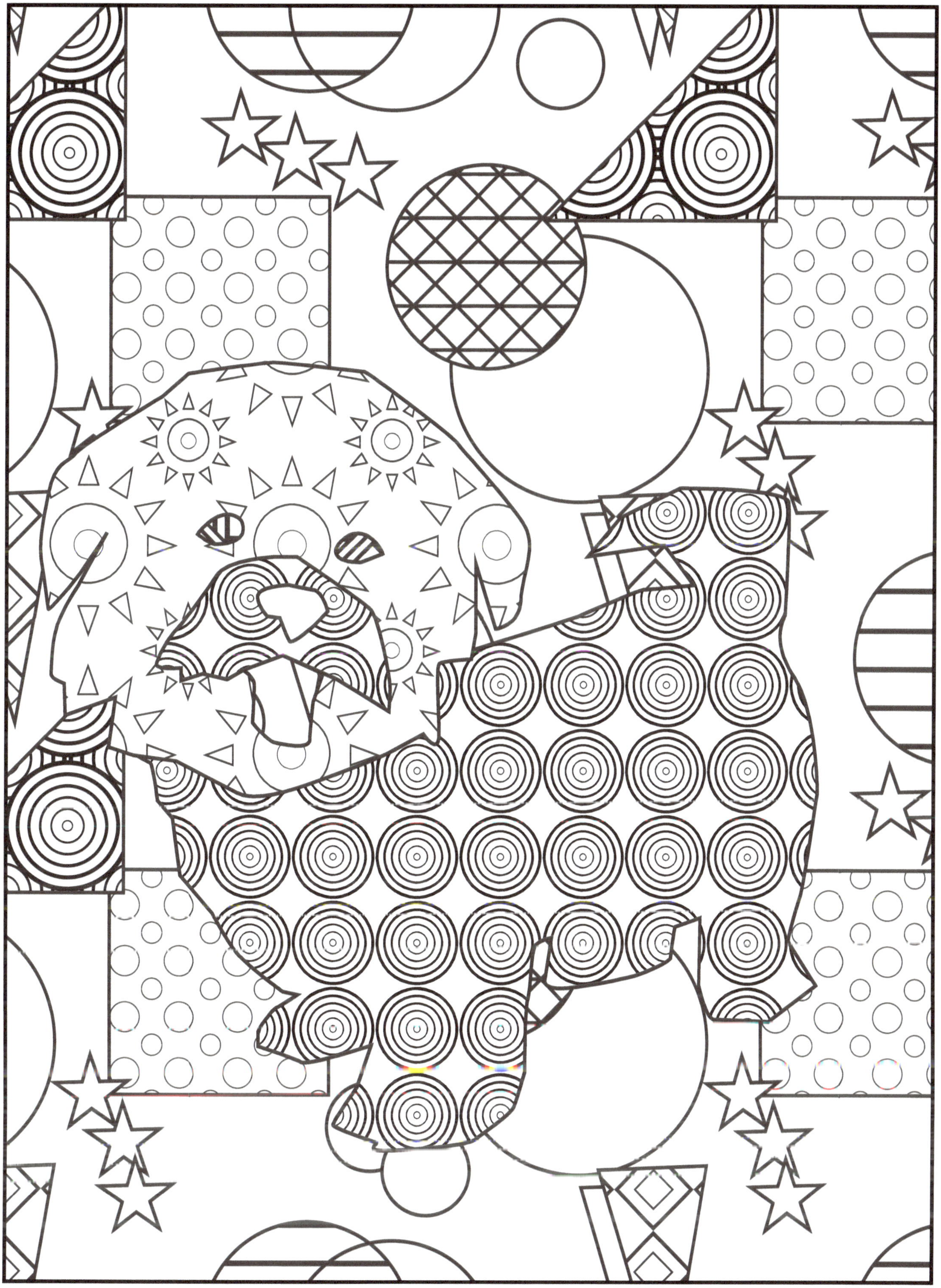

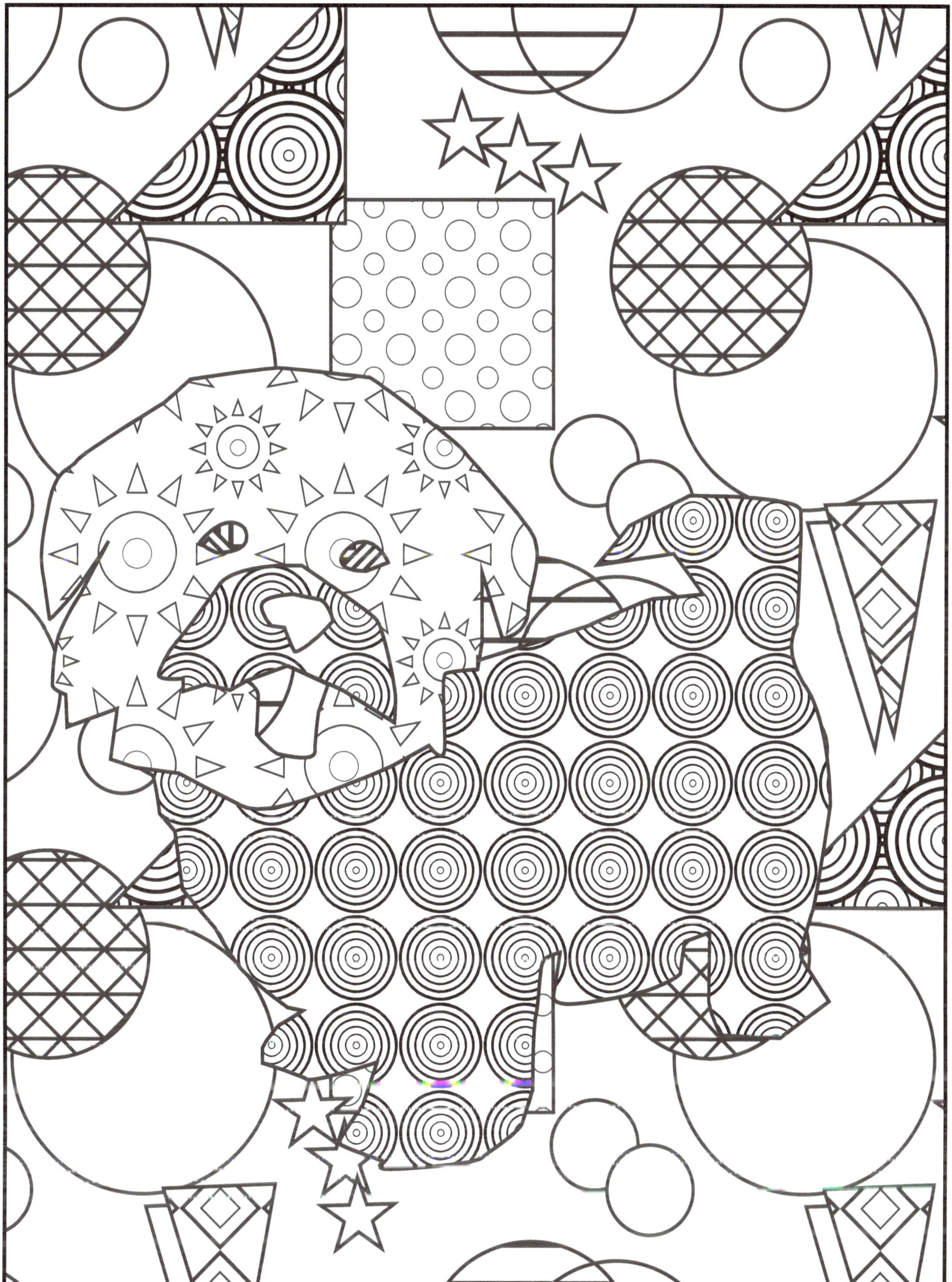

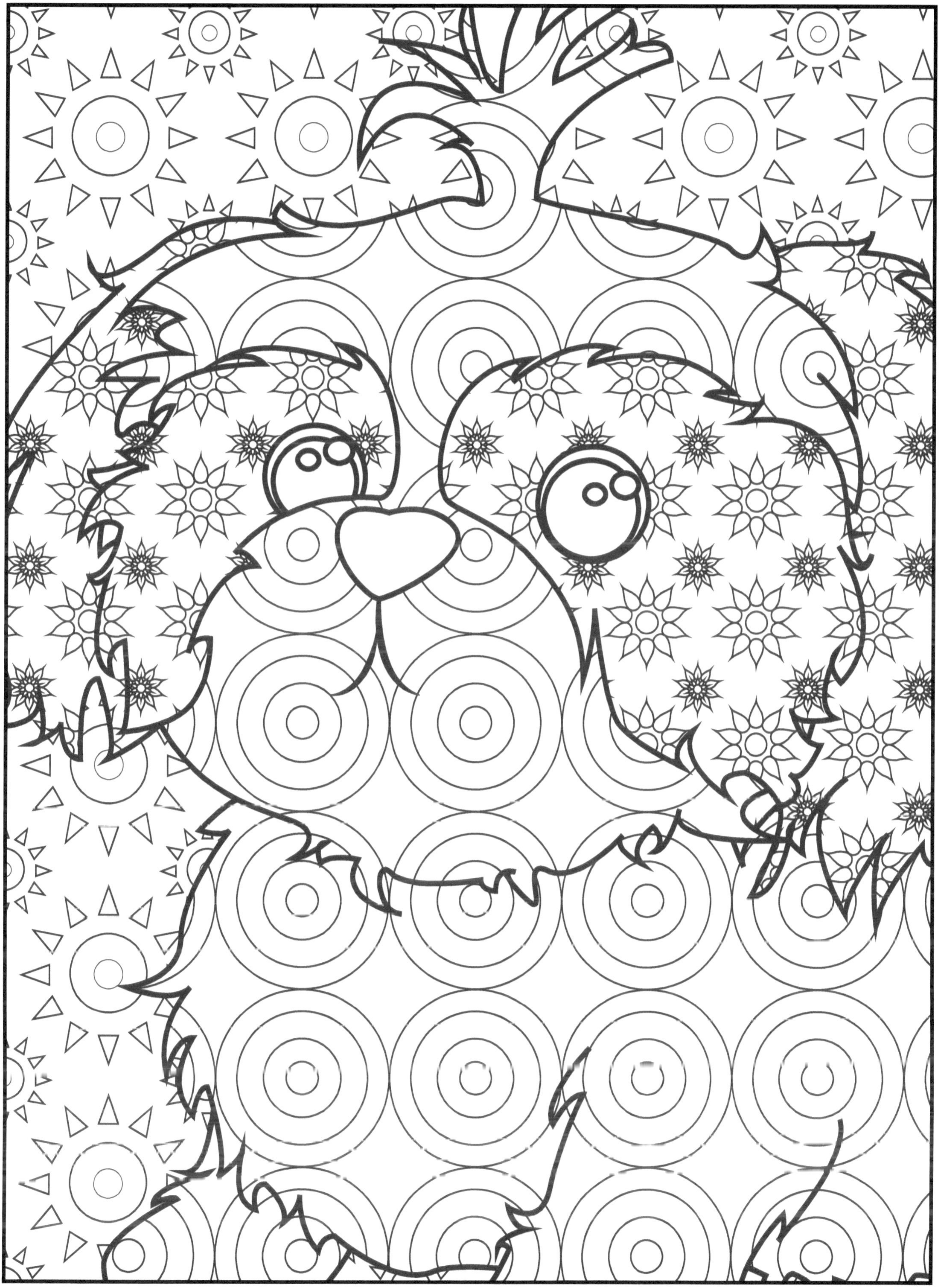

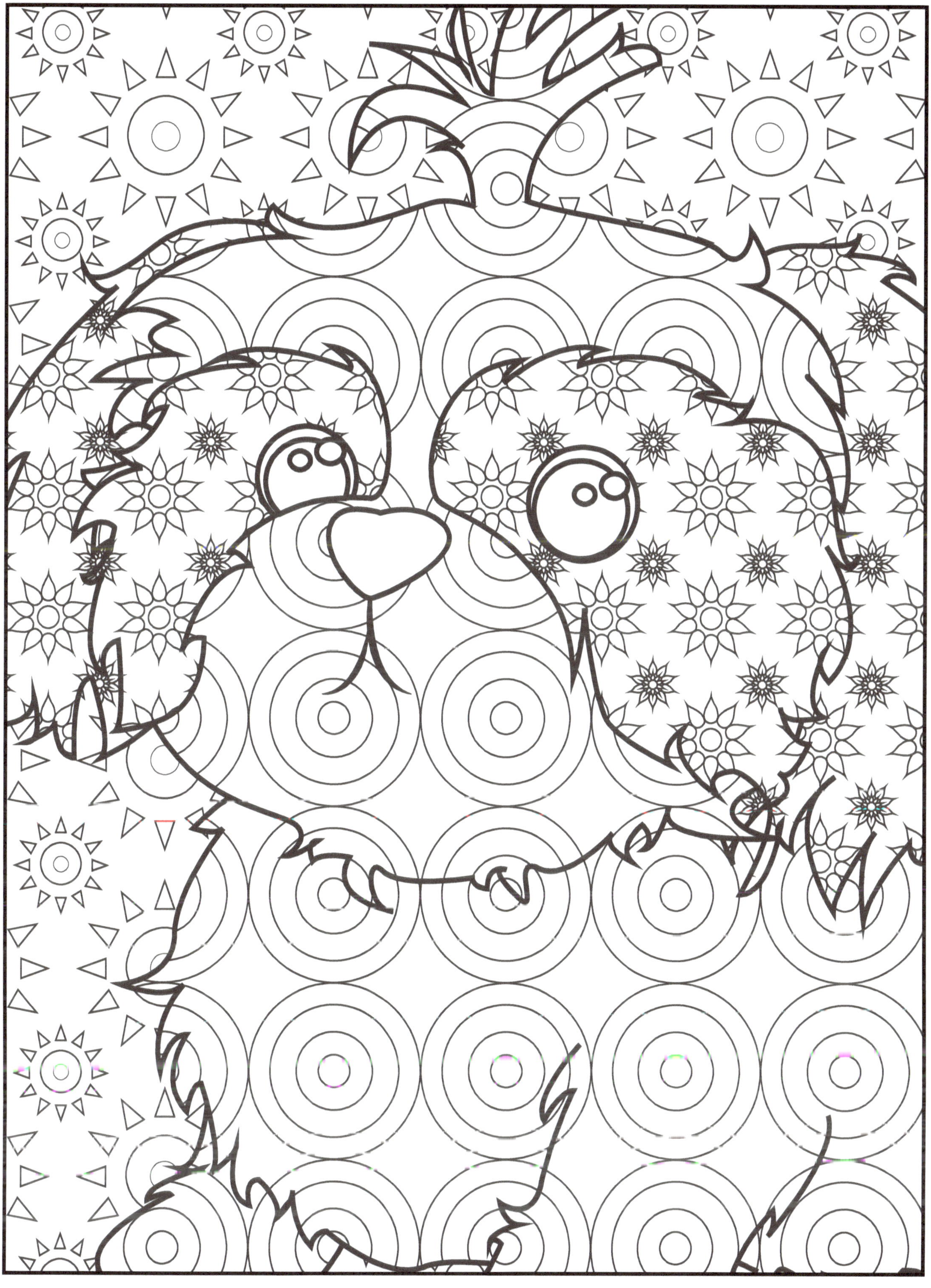

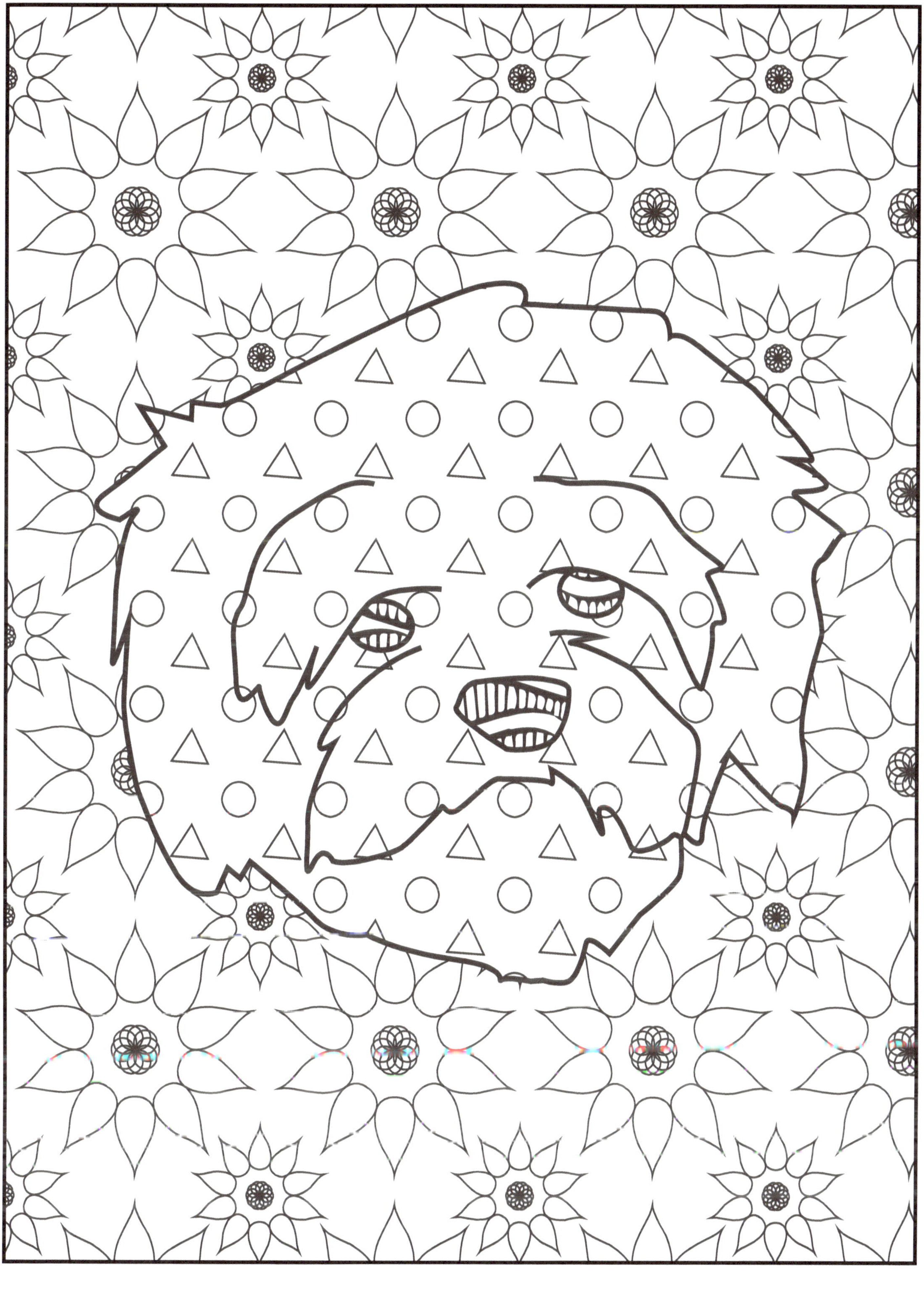

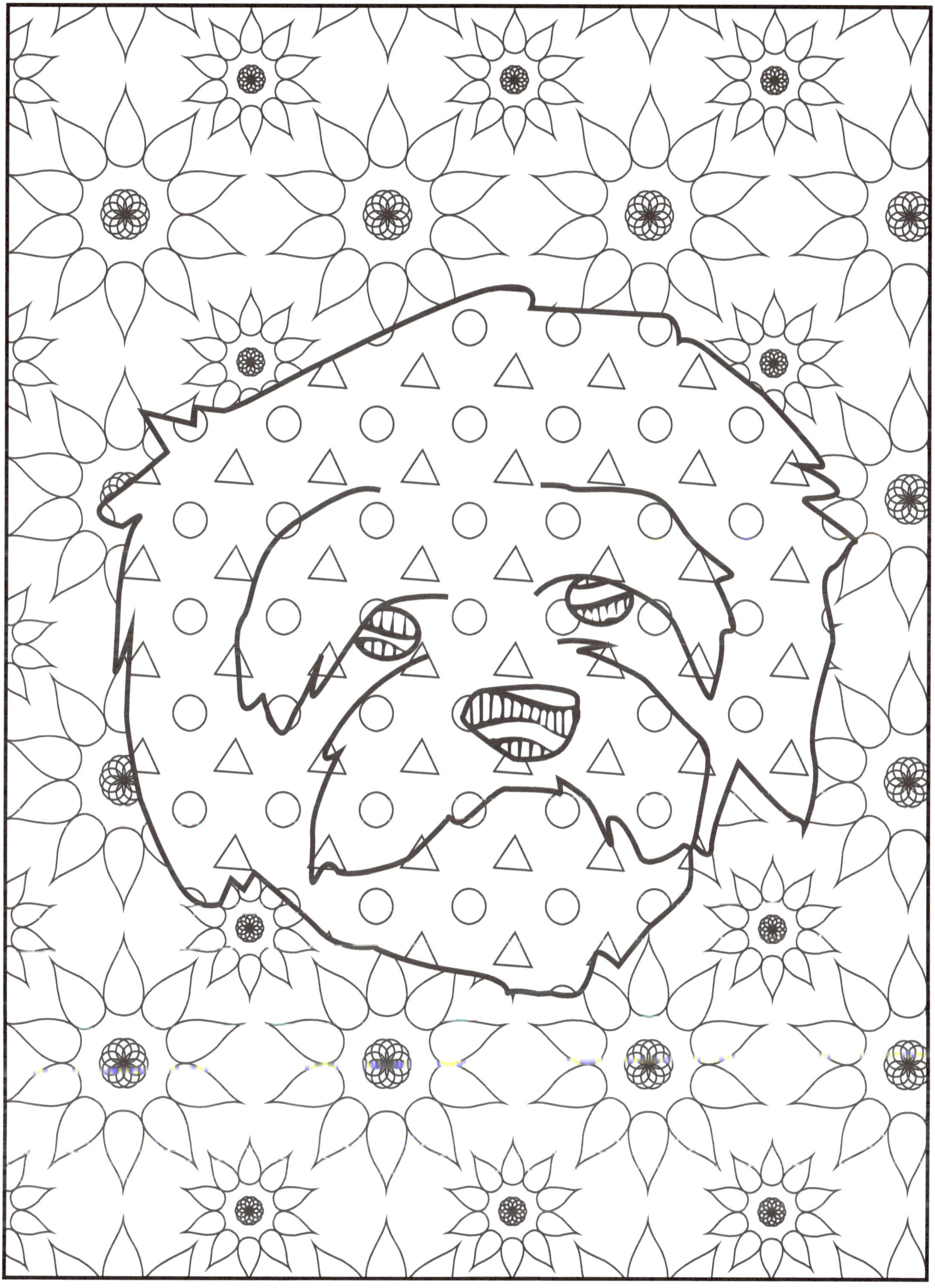

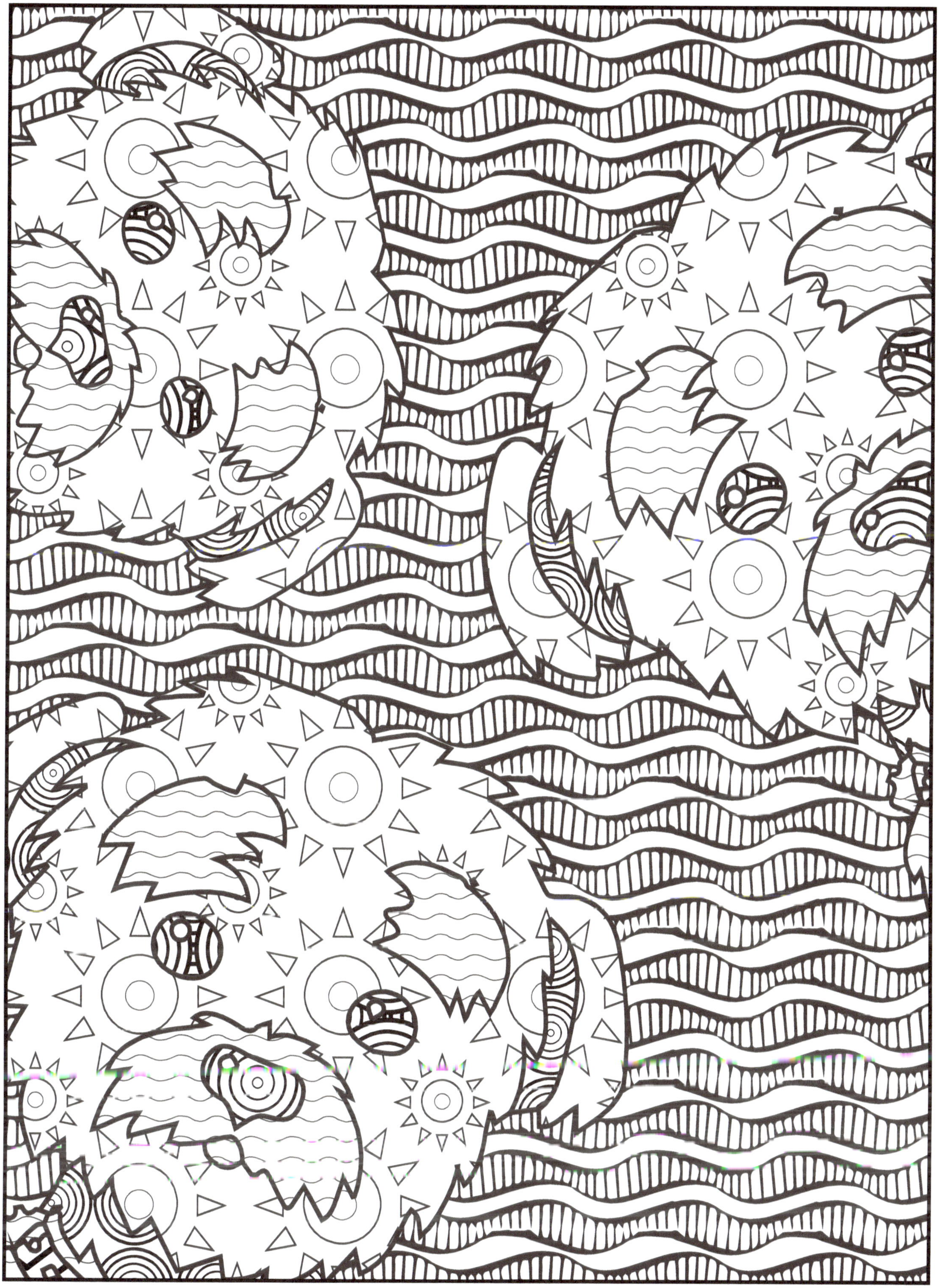

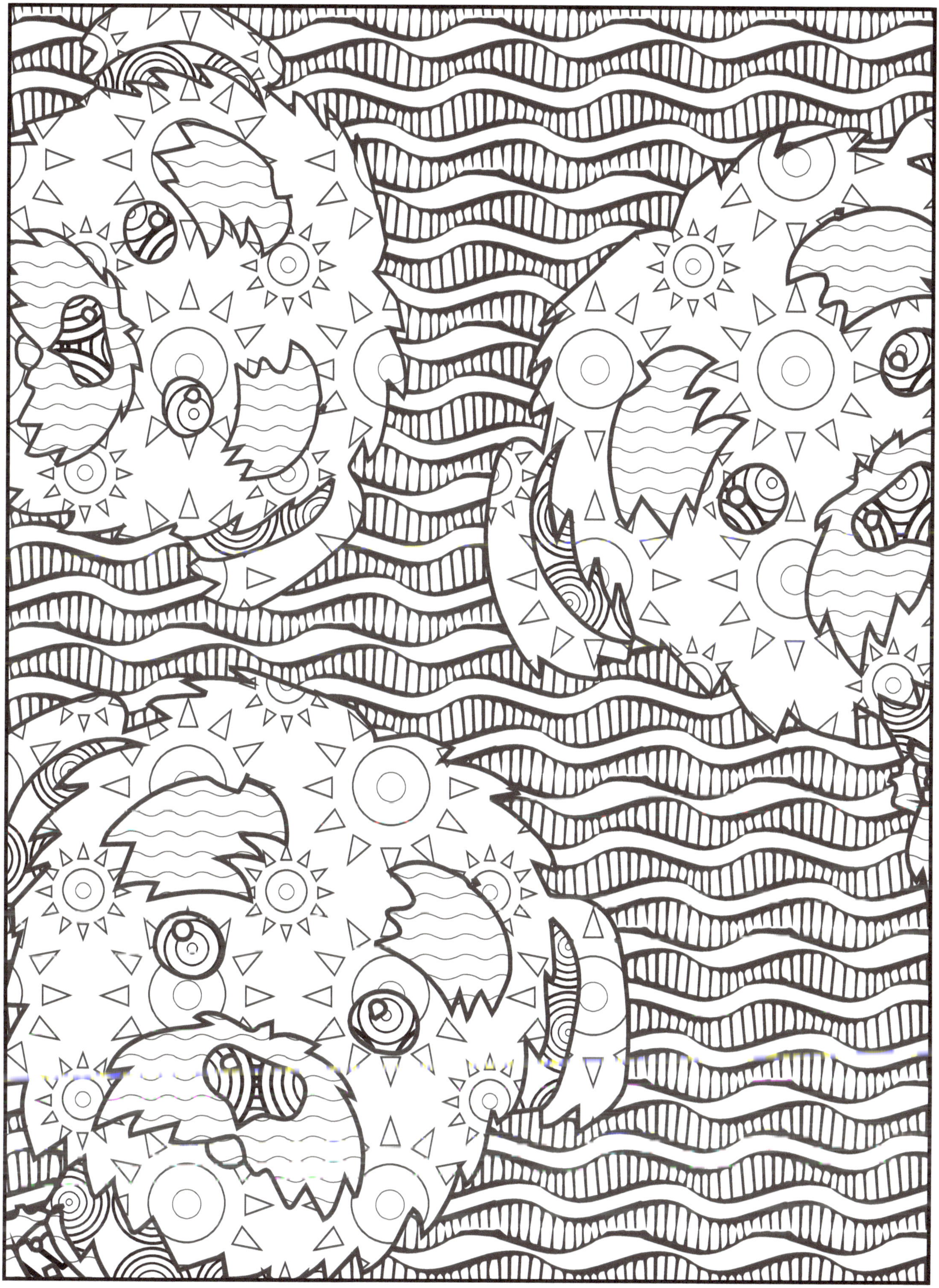

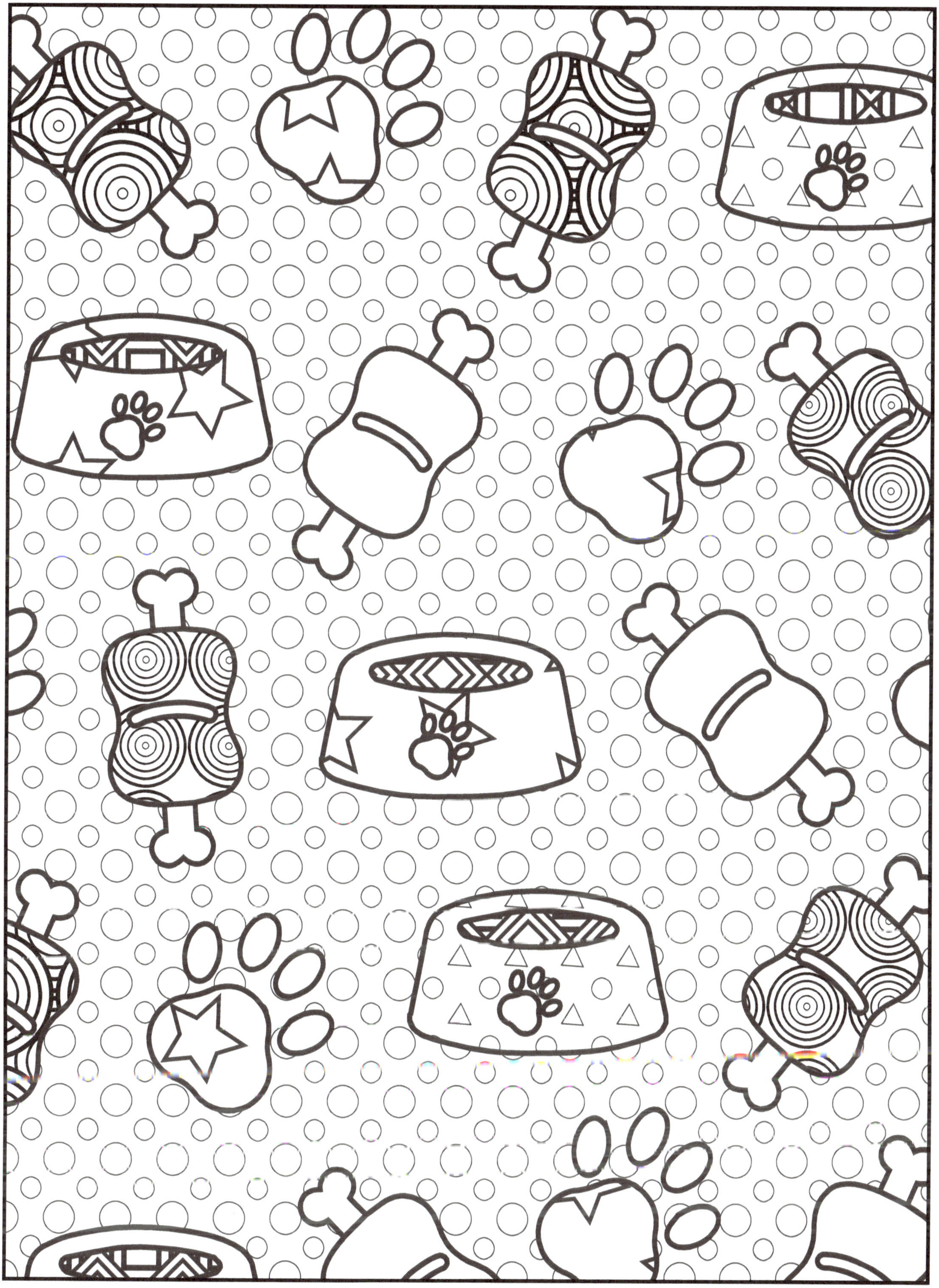

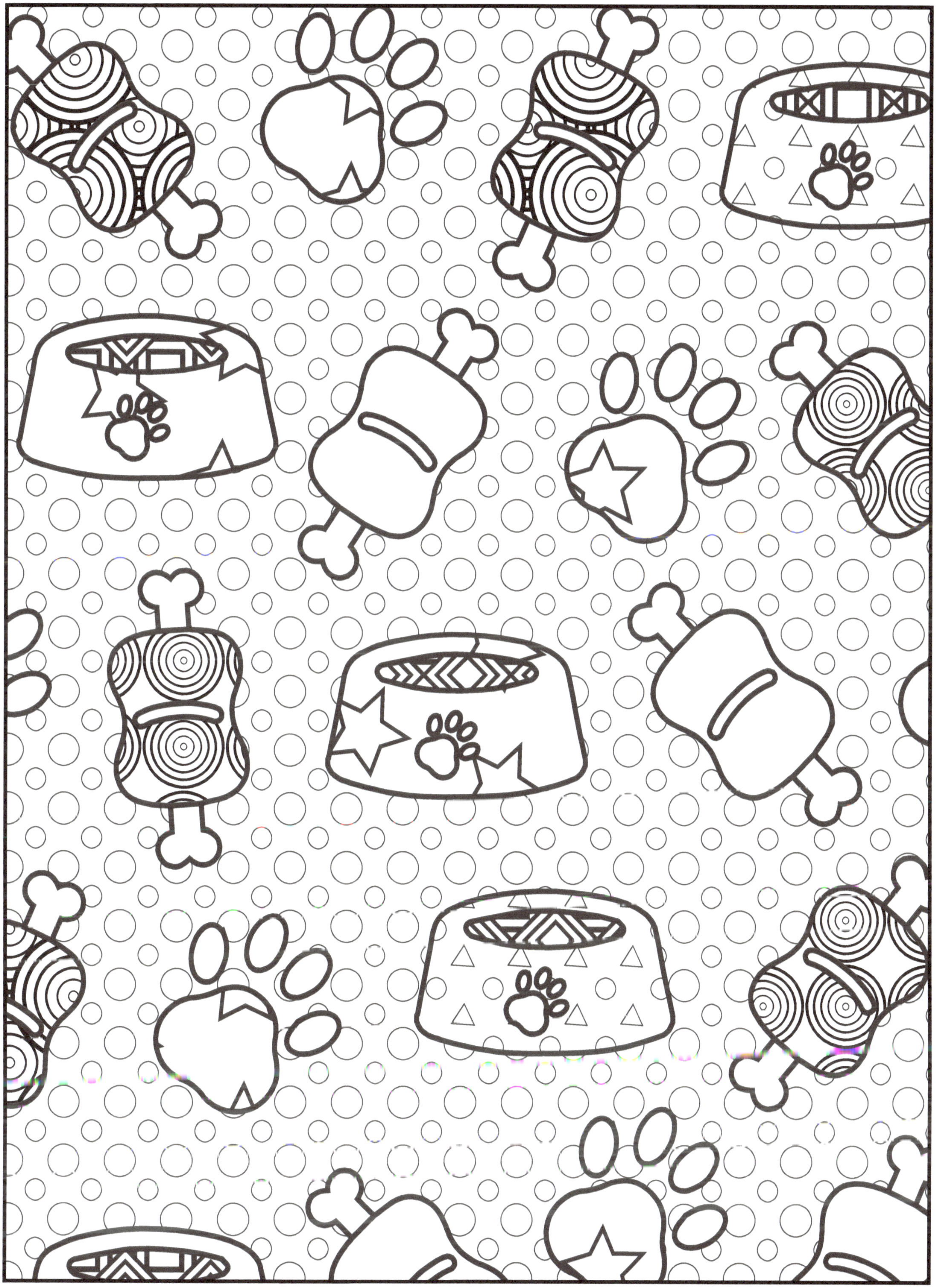

Made in United States
Troutdale, OR
08/08/2023

11896462R00038